Date Due

Oct 16

Bernard Soleul
101 W 55 St
N. Y. C.

READING THE NOVEL

READING THE NOVEL

BY

ELIZABETH CHRISTINE COOK, Ph.D.

OF TEACHERS COLLEGE
COLUMBIA UNIVERSITY

BOSTON
LITTLE, BROWN, AND COMPANY
1933

Copyright, 1933,
By Elizabeth Christine Cook

———

Not to your memory alone,
Mother,
but to you,
I offer this little book,
"if mine, then yours."

FOREWORD

The question of the reader's attitude towards reading has become steadily more important with the complexity of modern life. The habit of reading in a variety of ways can be fostered in the approach to novels, with their immense range from the shocker to the masterpiece. Hence this book has been undertaken in the hope that suggestions growing out of work among students at Teachers College, Columbia University, may have a broader usefulness.

I wish to acknowledge the kind suggestions of Professor Franklin T. Baker, of Professor Allan Abbott, and of Professor Frank McMurry on the general theme. Also my very sincere appreciation goes to the valuable help of Dr. Ella Woodyard of the Department of Psychology, Teachers College, Columbia University.

CONTENTS

READING THE NOVEL

CHAPTER I

SOME DISTINGUISHED READERS — THEIR RANGE AND SPEED, WITH HINTS AS TO THEIR METHODS

There is no tradition more ancient and hoary with respectability than the notion that to be slow means to be sure. Reinforced by maxim and precept, fitted to the pace of the dullest in droning schools of the past, this idea has been rolling up error like a snowball. It was fostered too, for generations, by the scarcity of books and the consequent natural desire to draw out every possible thought from any particular book. A book was an event. It must be made to last as long as possible. Of course there have been libraries belonging to renowned scholars and writers ever since the classical manuscript collections; and great writers have usually been wide readers. A scholar like Francis Bacon could easily discover the difference between books to be tasted and books to be swallowed. But these treasured libraries until recent times have been

Until recent days it has been considered creditable to read slowly

as inaccessible to the ordinary citizen as a king's chests of old. Even comparatively recent biographies again and again recite the list of the few books known in the families of a Franklin, a Whittier, a Lincoln, even a Stevenson. These few books were known by heart, always, and no others were known as a rule. Re-reading of very simple matter was regarded as admirable.

Picture for a moment the eighteenth-century English gentleman reading on the terrace of his country seat. Instead of the restless hum of motors on the road below, he hears only the occasional creak of a farm wagon, or the very occasional rumble of a family coach. No liveried footman comes out to tell him that the town office is on the wire. London is three good days away, with mails uncertain. It might be burning or otherwise devastated while still he reads peacefully in his *Sir Charles Grandison* and finally marks the place carefully before tea. So for many days, months, years, he has time for the seven volumes of *Sir Charles Grandison*, the eight volumes of *Clarissa Harlowe*, the two volumes of *Tristram Shandy*, the four volumes of *Pamela*. The very length of the eighteenth-century novel tells the story. It was meant to last, to be a solid source of mental nourishment and relaxation for years. Naturally,

Illustration in novel-reading of the eighteenth century

4

it was to be taken seriously, to be read word for word, without the frivolity of skipping even a single entanglement of the unhappy Clarissa. These books imply very slow reading, and they assume sure, thorough reading as a natural consequence.

Such assumptions have controlled standards in school reading until recent years. In other words, no form of reading except study was generally recognized. Even now one sometimes hears that old adage that any book which is worth reading at all is worth reading with attention to every detail, from cover to cover. Skipping, or even skimming, was regarded as a superficial, scatter-brained habit. When "English" as a special subject was established about fifty years ago the older modes of study of the classics practically dominated liberal education both in England and in the United States. Was it not very natural that the ideal in the minds of educators who first put the native literature into the schools should be to make it, like Latin, "sound and hard"? Something to justify its existence, they wished, as every new subject has to fight its way into the curriculum. English studies must be proved good discipline. And discipline they certainly became. The Latin lesson was the model. Many of us can remember the close, textual study of dainty little lyrics in

Former standards of reading in the schools

5

our mother tongue, the omnipresent dictionary, the mastery (including the derivation) of difficult and rare words, with no guessing, under pain of being regarded as a shifty improviser. The close study of individual paragraphs followed, with the outlining of chapters about Robin Hood and Friar Tuck, the technique of climax and dénouement applied to the fighting passages in *Ivanhoe*. Many of us have taught children to diagram the tournament at Ashby as if it were the latest world-map. There are still schools where *Ivanhoe* consumes weeks, and where Stevenson's *Travels with a Donkey* takes on an even slower rate of travel in the classroom. Is it surprising that we have trained two generations of students to whom literature read in the schools is often definitely distasteful?

Let us examine, for a moment, what happens in the older type of Latin study. I say "older type" because it is already giving way to methods which would once have been called cheating! Using a translation? Guessing by context? The dictionary too slow? These new heresies are transforming even a foreign language into something more rapidly familiar. But when, in the older method, supposedly more thorough, we have pieced every sentence together with the utmost care, so that we know the relation

One defect in such slowness

6

of every noun, and of every treacherous participle, it is still possible to miss the trend and meaning of the whole. How many of us, I wonder, can look back to student days and recall meeting an old friend, say an oration of Cicero, in a good translation, and realizing as our eyes swept rapidly along the text in our mother tongue, "Why, is *that* what it was all about"? Yet we had known every single word of it. We had simply missed the larger whole of the thought. There had been no perspective in our reading, no relating of values, no proportion. Everything lay on a flat plane. One object was just as important as another. The details were not held on a thread of purpose, nor theme, but were studied for their own sake, scattered and apart. The very time it consumes to read everything in this manner tends to scatter attention. We have to make many returns to the material, instead of taking it in one absorbing period.

Needless to say, reading standards are now changing very rapidly in the schools, with the corps of trained investigators at work on every aspect of the subject. But the practices and skills and habits in the reading world outside have been far in advance of changes in the schools. Early in the nineteenth century, the penny magazine brought

Changes in novel-reading in the nineteenth century

7

novels to every door in serial form. Dickens sometimes had several novels on the grill, in this way, at
one time. Now when a story is served up piece-
meal, we never have quite so much respect for the
different parts as we have for the bound volume.
Moreover, it is easy to skip or lose a number. Readers made the amazing discovery that they could
bridge gaps for themselves, and get on with the
new numbers. Books of all sorts became cheaper.
Reading became something like a universal art in
all civilized countries. And with this change, the
amount of reading material to be covered by the
reader of intelligence, whether in science, history,
practical arts, or *belles-lettres*, has increased by leaps
and bounds. A book has long since ceased to be a
treasure in, and for, itself. It comes with its very
jacket bidding for our attention: in color, in form,
and in crowded advertisements, — "blurb", — to
use the term of the trade. We pick and choose from
a flooded market. All these facts have increased
speed and extent in reading.

Certainly the reading covered by men and women
of achievement tends to be little short of astonishing
in range and amount. In our emphasis upon actual
achievement today, instead of upon theory, the
reading of practised readers becomes of more suggestive value to us than oceans of speculative method.

8

Just as the art of writing is more and more studied from those who have practised it rather than from medieval rhetorical theory, so we are be- **Reading** ginning to ask men and women of note in **habits of** the world of letters, of science, or of affairs **men and** how they read; when they skim over the **women of** pages, when they skip material, when they **achieve-** slow down, when they pause for reflection, **The ques-** when they re-read, when they actually **tions** study, learn, or memorize. How much **involved** do they discard or ignore altogether? Are they likely to know what they are reading for? More or less exactly what do they expect to get out of it? How do the best critics of literature proceed? How many novels can a good reviewer usually handle in an evening? in a week? and how does he do it? How far should his standards govern the student reader, and how far should the ordinary reader depart from them? Such are a few of the questions which we are beginning to put. And the first striking fact, as already indicated, is the wide range and amount of reading covered in general, by people of marked distinction in every walk of life.

It is natural enough to think of writers and scholars in *belles-lettres*, or in history, as very much at home in their libraries. We do not feel any surprise that Thackeray was widely read, even to the point of

9

scholarship in eighteenth-century English manners and customs. We have long been familiar with the

I. In the field of literature careful reading and study which George Eliot put upon Florence in the days of Savonarola before writing her novel *Romola*, not to mention her wide readings in the philosophy of Comte and others. There was no medieval legend too deeply buried in dusty bookstalls for Robert Browning to dig up and bring to new life. Carlyle growled over no one knows how many tomes before he produced his *Frederick the Great*. Any American reader must feel some shame at those easy references to Franklin, Cooper, Thoreau, which are found in the Russian novelists. Even Dickens, not known as a reader in adult life, pored over the volumes of Cervantes, Swift, Sterne, Goldsmith, Richardson, Defoe, Fielding, Smollett, when he was a delicate, bookish lad. Sometimes the reading recorded seems hardly credible in amount, as, for instance, in the case of Robert Louis Stevenson.

It is well to pause for a moment over Stevenson's reading, for in many ways he is the ideal reader.

a) **Stevenson** Books took on vivid personality for him from his first "shock of pleasure", as he calls it, in the silent reading of a book of fairy-tales while walking through a Scotch firwood. Here he first knew that he loved reading, and from that childish experience on through his life, he devoured books. The reading covered when he was between twenty-one and twenty-three years of age seems hardly possible, while the list he gives jauntily enough in his letters from Mentone on the Riviera, during the first illness, would be large enough for most of us in good health. Of course, *Don Quixote* and the novels of George Sand were mere bits of playtime with him. Taine and Clough were just convalescent diversion. He was writing on Victor Hugo for the *Cornhill Magazine* by 1874. He proposed to the Academy by January, 1875, a series of papers on the Parnassiens, — de Banville, Coppée, Soulary, and Prudhomme. The offer was not accepted, yet he read on in fifteenth-century French literature, until he produced his articles on Villon and Charles of Orléans, projecting others on the Maid, on Louis XI, and on René of Anjou. Meanwhile, he tried his hand at verse in the French metres of the fifteenth century, the ballade and the rondeau. For all these projects he read very widely, and was at the same time engaged in reading for other subjects. Yet Stevenson never let books master him, for their own sake. He kept a fine discrimination. He read hundreds of novels lightly enough. Yet he has his list of known and intimate friends among his books. These he read and re-read. Some of them he knew almost "by heart." And it is to be noted that he regarded works of fiction as the most influential of all, and that a few great novelists are on his very selected list, which we give below:

Victor Hugo	Hazlitt
Dumas	Burns
Scott	Herbert Spencer
George Sand	Heine
Meredith (The Egoist)	Keats
Defoe	Bunyan
Sterne	Thoreau
Fielding	Wordsworth
Thackeray	Whitman
Horace	Montaigne
Shakespeare	

And how is it with modern critics and reviewers of literature? If we look into the reading of a well-known critic, like the late James Gibbon Huneker, as he has left his rich records of it in varied memoirs and letters, the result is really bewildering to the ordinary, every-day reader. Here is a musical critic, first and foremost, who knows not only the composers, great and small, — Wagner, Chopin, Liszt, Strauss, and the rest, — but all the various authorities on them. He himself becomes an authority on

b) James Gibbon Huneker — His speed and range

Liszt, going into details about his life, taking a journey to Villa d'Este, Tivoli, to sleep at Liszt's hotel,
as well as to St. Francesco Kloster, where Liszt spent
his last days.   But this is only the beginning.   Huneker knew the interpreters of music just as well.   He
could write with sure feeling about Plante, Hummel,
Kisler, Pugno, Theodore Ritter, Colonne.   In addition Huneker was for years the well-known art
critic of *The Sun*, the first American critic to intro-
duce Cezanne, Gauguin, Friesz.   He knew the Italian Futurists as well as he knew Matisse, Picasso,
Monet, and could tell you at any moment what might
be upstairs at Durand Ruel's or at other galleries.
He was at home with the rarer works of Piranesi and
of Blake.   Add to this Huneker's knowledge of modern literature, especially drama, and we begin to have
a notion of the man's range.   He was not only writing on modern drama with a scope which took in
Ibsen, Hauptmann, Sudermann, Strindberg, Gorky,
D'Annunzio, the De Goncourts, Maeterlinck, Pinero,
Henri Becque, Villiers de l'Isle-Adam, Shaw, Yeats,
Hyde, Moore, Echegaray, but had his mental tele-
scope always sweeping the heavens for new stars, such
as "this new man, Artzibashev" about whom he
wrote a review for *The Sun* as early as 1914, and whose
books he kept on adding to his reading as fast as they
came out in either German or French, ten years or so

13

ahead of their translation into English. He could write a criticism of Bernard Shaw's *Man and Superman*, in which he showed the obligation of Shaw to Schopenhauer, Nietzsche, Voltaire, Swift, Vauvenargues, and others. Gautier, Balzac, Flaubert, Baudelaire are old friends to him. In one charming bit, Huneker described a visit to the little atelier of Flaubert, where he wrote *Madame Bovary*, at Croisset. Novels of all sorts were tucked into Huneker's spare moments. He was not only at once familiar with the newest output of Conrad, Wells, or Chesterton, but knew the authors themselves as a most favored reviewer might. He had a memorable day with Joseph Conrad at his country seat in Kent.

And how was it all done? Unfortunately, in his rushing life, which included the rapid writing of his *c) Huneker's methods and the technique of reviewers in general* own short stories as well as everything else we have mentioned, Huneker does not set down for us his technique of approach. We have to infer it from hints here and there. Often he does speak of skimming a new book which he regards as of less than first-rate importance. He takes a long novel like Mrs. Wharton's *House of Mirth* at a single sitting. Yet Huneker is not superficial, as his comments on the *House of Mirth* amply prove. His speed does not seem to be due so much to skipping as

14

to a rapid seizure of the text before him, with all the rich, apperceptive basis which he could always bring to it. We read with what we have read before. Then, too, a reviewer reads with the time mark ahead of him. This fact may make for superficiality, but it certainly also shows that we could all probably go much faster than we do. The reviewer who found the *Cycle of Adams Letters* so interesting that he read each of the large volumes through in a night was probably not endowed with extraordinary speed. He had cultivated it. On the other hand, the practice of reading two or three novels in an evening, for review, has led to the well-known joke about the reviewer who said that he felt himself unequal to reviewing a particular book, because he happened to have read it. Perhaps the ordinary reviewing practice of seizing the opening situation in a novel, then striking boldly into the middle or the second half for the dramatic centre, with a look at the conclusion, can hardly be called reading. Yet it gives a surprisingly complete grasp of the mere story, and may be useful for certain purposes, as we shall see in a later chapter.

The scientist tends to read with less cosmopolitan scope than the man or woman of letters, yet it is remarkable to see how carefully, as a rule, he controls the whole output of his subject and of collateral related subjects as well. Dr. E. L. Thorndike has told us that the creative mind is generally eager to know the researches, the ideas, and the range of others in the field. It would seem as though early reading in many cases was the very stimulus to awaken and guide later work. It is significant that Dr. Darwin, father of Charles Darwin, was the founder of the Derby Philosophical Society, and encouraged the boy's interests, not only in out-of-door nature study, but in scientific books and periodicals. The young Charles Darwin always carried a book with him, and covered the known science of his day before embarking on any of his own experiments and voyages. One cannot look into the memoirs and letters of a Huxley, or a Tyndall, without noticing trained and wide reading in their own fields. This reading, as a rule, means very careful attention to details and therefore a slower rate.

II. In the field of science

A notable exception would seem to be found in Herbert Spencer. He called himself a poor reader, conscientiously believed himself to be one from his school days, when he was rebuked for his hurry over the words by his schoolmaster uncle, who nevertheless remarked in the same breath that the boy's acquaintance with unusual words was extensive. He had gained this, without reading lessons, from the scientific periodical of that

a) **Herbert Spencer an exception? Prominence of the self in his reading**

16

same Derby Philosophical Society of which his father was secretary. But Herbert Spencer skipped a great deal, so he tells us, reading here and there as some phrase caught his eye. This trick followed him all through life. He was in haste to tear through a book for what he wanted, and then he immediately dropped it. His natural impatience accounts in part for this habit, but it is due largely to his powerful ego, which simply could not endure to sit under anyone else's thought, even on the printed page. So he read Kant until he felt a total disagreement with his philosophy and then stopped abruptly. George Eliot induced him to read the introduction to Comte's *Philosophie Positive*, but he read only far enough to disagree with Comte's classification of sciences. That was enough. His habitual expression for his relation with books is "dipping", or when it comes to novels, of which he was very fond, "scrambling." Obviously, Spencer was ultra-modern, a self-trained skipper, touching the high spots. He shows very clearly in his work the dangers of the habit, particularly for a scientist. If Spencer had subjected himself to more patient, exact discipline in his reading acquaintance with science as known in his day, he might not have been so dogmatically sure that acquired character can be inherited, nor so fond of projecting a whole universe complete in all details

17

according to his own notions. The most amusing bit of arrogance in his *Autobiography* is the account of his attempt to read Plato, and his disgust at the thinker and his dummy, although Spencer admits that there are in Plato detached thoughts from which he might benefit if he had patience.

In other words, Spencer read with such a prominence of the self, and of the interest of the moment, that his preconceived ideas never got out of his way for any impersonal, cool, scientific attitude towards what he read. His ego was always there. In the sense that it always told him what he wanted to get, it prevented his ever becoming slavish or mechanical in covering ground merely for the sake of an exacting erudition. This is a fine point for the average reader to note. Spencer valued his text only if it stimulated his own thinking, suggested illuminating new ideas or points of view. He is constantly referring to some phrase found in his reading as fruitful in this way. Thus he became a creative reader, making his books take him further in his own thought, rather than provide any authority for him. Even though he is an extreme example of this mode, he can become very valuable to us in showing us purposeful reading, related to the self.

Spencer never studied anything outside his own systems, or outside his own immediate wants. Yet he had a remarkable grasp of material, with all his impatient seizure of it, and he quotes with familiarity from a wide range of thinkers, workers, teachers, and writers, not only in science, but in education. He knew Pestalozzi, Horace Mann, Fellenberg, Marcel, Bernard, the Battersea School Reports, etc. He was familiar with Emerson, Mill, Faraday, Holmes, Thackeray, and a host of others. Another point which stands out for the average reader is Spencer's use of his spare moments in reading. Much of this large amount he covered almost in passing, as it were, in spare moments, at a prodigious rate. When he was too tired for any other work, he "scrambled" through a novel. Novels he enjoyed for rest and refreshment, and he read many of them. Here too is a suggestion for the general reader. Spencer knew how to take his freshest hours for concentrated, rapid study, and to read a story in an entirely different, relaxed, easy manner with even less conscience.

An instance of rather wide reading where we should not expect it is found in our own engaging, popular naturalist, John Burroughs. Reared on a *b)* John Catskill farm with access to only forty or Bur-fifty district-library books such as *Murphy,* roughs *the Indian Killer,* with no reading in his home, with all his preferences for out-of-door life, with his long seasons at Slabsides in the woods, he would not seem likely to be a voluminous reader. And, of course, in comparison with a Macaulay or a Carlyle, he was a smatterer in books. Yet the simplest glance at the Burroughs memoirs shows a reading knowledge of Aristotle, Epictetus, Bacon, Huxley, Fabre, Bergson, Tennyson, Whitman, Maeterlinck, Carlyle, Parkman, Boswell, Darwin, Eckerman, Wordsworth, Bryant, White's *Natural History of Selborne*, Thoreau, John Muir, Irving, Hawthorne, Goldsmith, Barrie, Shakespeare, Pope, Johnson, Lowell, and, of course, Emerson. History and science he delighted in, though he, too, was a good novel reader in spare moments, giving his special attention to the novels of his friend Howells, whom he admired greatly. Burroughs read slowly, however, with no modern training in the matter. The surprising thing is to see the range and extent of his reading.

The distinction between the man of action and the **III. In the world of affairs — a) Alexander the Great and Julius Caesar** man of thought is an ancient one, fostered by our natural enjoyment of dramatic moments in the careers of famous men. Every school child has the picture of Alexander the Great weeping for more worlds to conquer. How many realize that he carried his secretaries with him into Asia, not only to make him famous, but because of his love of philosophy and books? How many ever

think of Julius Caesar as a man of letters except, perhaps, for an unwilling memory of "All Gaul is di-
vided into three parts"? Most of us would find it
hard to imagine the racing speed with which the
scribes took Caesar's dictation of his commentaries,
in spare moments wedged in between crises affecting
the history of the Western world. The compression
of style shows how Caesar packed all he could into
a given space. He wrote books on language and
grammar, no one knows when or how. As to his
reading, he not only had a perfect mastery of Greek,
knowing the Greek historians and poets in the original, but he was so versed in the literary criticism of
his day that Cicero praises him as a man of letters.
When the two men were politically opposed, they
could meet on common ground for purely literary and
linguistic talks as they did in the Saturnalia vacation
of 45 B.C., at Cicero's villa on the Bay of Naples, near
Puteoli. Although we cannot know directly just
how Caesar did his reading, we can safely infer that
he covered the ground with tremendous rapidity in
his few moments or hours between military and
political events. He could never have done it in
any other way. The fact that he did it at all has
been half-buried and forgotten in his life of crowded
action. One thing, however, we do know. We have
Cicero's authority for the statement that Caesar

always carried a note-book with him, a commonplace book in which he put down anything of note in his reading or his conversation with others. We know, too, that his reading became a part of his experience. When he crossed the Rubicon, he quoted a phrase from Menander's tragedy *Arrephoros*, "Let the die be cast."

Above all, who ever recalls that Napoleon had 800 books with him *at the Battle of Waterloo?* So excel-
b) Na- lent an authority as Lord Rosebery vouches
poleon for this. And whether this precise fact be legendary or not, certain it is that Napoleon read often, and widely. He used a book, however, just as he used everything else, in a high-handed, cavalier manner. If it displeased him, or if he was done with it, he simply threw it out of his coach window, literally strewing his way over Europe with discarded volumes. No stately library with the treasured bindings of first editions for him. A book was just an instrument to serve him for what he wanted at the moment. It might be well to gain something of this high-handed attitude, as indeed our modern education for use, for service, tends to do. At the same time we need not lose our love for the selected, chosen library of our life-long book-friends. Many books to be used; some books to stay with us.

Gladstone's study of Greek when he was over eighty has been sufficiently striking to be coupled with Cato's. His library, his reading in- *c)* **Glad-** terests have long been well known. We **stone and** know Disraeli as the author of *Vivian Grey* **Disraeli** and other Byronic novels, but do we often realize that he almost became a scholar, buried in the library, as his father had been? His wide acquaintance with books, especially with the legislators, poets, and philosophers of modern Europe at a time when the classics held the field in education, his remarkable knowledge of geography and history, English and foreign, were to serve him well when he planned an empire and achieved it. One pleasant little side light on his early ability to read very rapidly is found in the story of his reading romances beside a schoolfellow only six months younger, who was so much slower in his reading that Benjamin Disraeli good-naturedly waited at each page for his companion to finish before turning the leaf, since they had only one volume between them. Doubtless the tact and patience gained in such ways served as excellent preparation for his later dealings with celebrated personages also of less intelligence than himself. Disraeli was always a confirmed reader of romances and novels.

Americans have reason for some pride in the wide reading, the very large range, of at least two among

23

the founders of the republic, — men of action in every sense, as well as of thought. Benjamin Franklin was always an indefatigable reader, poring over his few volumes as a boy, importing books from England for his printing office later on. He printed the first American edition of *Pamela*, in 1744, when it was daring public opinion to bring out any novel whatever in the American Colonies. The book notices in those days included chiefly titles like these:

d) Benjamin Franklin — Range and extent of reading

Twenty Considerations against Sin
Catechistical Guide to Sinners
The dreadful Sound with which the Wicked are to be
    Thunderstruck
The Day of a Godly Man's Death Better than the Day
    of his Birth
Tract on Anabaptist Plunging
A short plain Help for Parents to Feed their Babes with
    the Sincere Milk of God's Word

The difficulty in getting hold of literature of any sort in the colonies was very great. The well-known private libraries contained, for the most part, Latin works of theology. We can therefore imagine what a love of reading secular literature made Franklin import the English novels of his day, along with a large number of classics. He established the first informal subscription library in America. Even a partial list of what he knew and read, self-taught in his earlier years, will be impressive if we remember what each title represents. Often the Harvard library of the period did not possess these volumes of *belles-lettres* which Franklin managed to buy, beg, borrow, or publish.

Virgil	Epictetus
Aristotle	Plutarch
Shakespeare	Cicero
Milton	Plato
Addison's *Spectator*	Horace
Swift's *Tale of a Tub*	Congreve
Cowley	Sallust
Robinson Crusoe	Juvenal
Moll Flanders	Persius
Pamela	Butler's *Hudibras*
The Tatler	Cato's Letters
The Guardian	Ovid
Don Quixote	Otway's Plays
Steele's Plays	Pembroke's *Arcadia*
Dryden	Prior
Waller	Rowe's *Lucan*
Rowe	Seneca's *Morals*
Pope	*Select Novels*, 6 volumes
Voltaire	Rabelais, 4 volumes

Arbuthnot	Bunyan
Bacon	*Cynthia, A Novel*
Locke	*The Republic of Letters*
Shaftesbury	*The Garden of Love*
Gay	*The Ladies' Delight*
Spenser	*Fair Rosamond*
Xenophon	

We see even from this partial list, which is a fragmentary indication from his early advertisements and catalogues, that Franklin enjoyed the novels and plays of his day with hearty relish. Yet his main interests were always in applied science. It would be impossible even to indicate what he absorbed in this field, before experimenting with the lightning. Enough that he devoured books greedily all his long life. He regarded a book as his safest debauch, snug and quiet. Often he read far into the night, or shortened his lunch to finish some treatise. As a poor runaway apprentice he carried so many books that the Governor of New York heard of it, and invited the lad to come for a talk in the Governor's library. Years afterwards, when Dr. Franklin returned from his active, cosmopolitan life in France, he brought with him eighteen large boxes of books for which he had to enlarge his library in Philadelphia, already one of the largest, if not the largest library in the country.

How did Franklin read? For the most part, we shall have to infer his methods. For one thing, he read with the absorbed attention which Franklin's made it a kind of dissipation. He always method of describes it in terms of an orgy. This reading means, of course, that not a second of his reading time was wasted in scattered thoughts. Often he had borrowed a book which had to be returned the next morning. It was always finished. The additional concentration of speed was necessary. Furthermore, his life, from his early years, was crowded with action, with stirring events in which he had a major part. It would have been a sheer impossibility to cover the amount of reading he did, in spare moments, unless he had developed great speed. Yet he advised a woman friend to keep a notebook for entering hints and impressions; in short to read with pen in hand for the purpose; even to use a dictionary for the difficult terms in science. He probably referred to helps for beginners, although he himself undoubtedly could study a text in this way if he thought it wise to do so. This habit of using the little "commonplace book" for entering useful quotations and hints from one's reading seems to be very common among distinguished readers.

Franklin read almost everything that came to hand, especially in his earlier years of poverty. He could not pick and choose to any extent. We do not expect to find any ordered system in his reading, until he reached his researches in applied science and philosophy. Even these were much interrupted. He often sighed for more time to carry on his "philosophical studies." But Thomas Jefferson could read with masterly system from the first. He could afford to send to England for costly books. If we should erase from his record every political and diplomatic achievement, we should have left a very considerable name as a scholar, an architect, a philosopher, and a daring thinker in education. Master of Greek, Latin, French, and English, at home in Italian, Spanish, and Anglo-Saxon, he began his reading as soon as he could see the hands of the clock in the morning, while after the candles were brought in at Monticello he usually read on through the evening, scarcely moving in his study chair. As a college student he read about fifteen hours a day. Although he shared to the full in the classical revival, and was dominated on the whole by classical ideals, he took up Anglo-Saxon when it was very exceptional to do so, and earnestly wished it emphasized at the University of Virginia along with modern languages. He could quote the Church fathers as fluently as those who called him

e) Thomas Jefferson — The range of his interests, his scholarship

28

an infidel, and as a matter of course always had an array of classic authors at his finger-tips. He could tilt with Buffon in Paris on questions in natural history, or at Monticello with Humboldt on philosophy. He was an authority on the agriculture of his day in Virginia. Add to all this his intense and constant reading in politics, his interest in music, his ability to draw his own plans for the pillared Monticello in the Italian manner of Palladio, and we shall begin to see the fertility of his power without even mentioning the Declaration of Independence, or the Presidency of the United States.

Fortunately Jefferson has left us some notes and hints as to his methods in reading. They are contained in the advice he gave to his younger friends, to his nephew, and to his grandson. The system which guided his own reading clearly emerges from the outlines he made out for them. In the first place he believed in mapping it all out into a definite course, covering a particular subject, in a particular way, and never allowing one's self to deviate from the plan until it had been carried out. No by-paths, no dissipating of time and energy, by scattered attention. Along with this, he implied clearly that one should choose a particular course of reading very purposefully, for certain definite training, or for needed knowledge,

Jefferson's method of reading

29

cultivation, or recreation. He not only used a precise clock schedule himself, but always advised it. Know where you are, and what you are doing, and what time it is, and whether you are falling short of your schedule or not, and how far short. It is clear that this was what he made himself do in all matters and particularly in his reading. We know that this constant, deliberate consciousness of the clock tends to efficient speed and prevents dawdling, unless it becomes a restless, nervous habit, a kind of wristwatch mania which defeats its own end. Jefferson's speed was always calm, even stately, like the tick of a tall mahogany clock. But it was fast, nevertheless, with no false steps, no jerks of uncertainty, no flapping over the pages. Progress was massive and real.

In his outlines and recommendations for reading and study he puts the hardest work always in the fresh morning hours, advising his young friends to read in anatomy, zoölogy, botany, chemistry, agriculture, and ethics, *until* eight o'clock in the morning, citing authors in the various sciences as then known. From eight to twelve the young law students whom he had in mind could read law, *taking care to enter every case of value into a commonplace book* for future reference and memory.

Jefferson's advice about reading

From twelve to one he would read politics, including Locke, Sidney, Montesquieu, Parliamentary Debates of England and Ireland, *The Federalist*, Malthus on *Population*, etc. Then, running on into the afternoon Jefferson would advise what he considered lighter reading; namely, the Greek and Latin historians in the original, along with modern history. Last of all, from candles to bedtime he would relax with *belles-lettres*, criticism, rhetoric. As a rule he read only the classics in literature. Shakespeare he admired, and a small list of novelists, — Fielding, Smollett, Sterne, Marmontel, Gil Blas, and Cervantes. It is said that he read *Don Quixote* more than once, a rare tribute from him. Of course, we must remember that his course of reading here given refers to the student's life. Undoubtedly it is the one he pursued himself as a student. He could not keep up anything like this in active life, but just so far as possible he retained these habits and methods. If the result seems impossible, we must remember that in the eighteenth century it was possible to cover in a general way the whole body of known science, philosophy, and history. We can observe, too, how without any school knowledge of psychology Jefferson believed in variety in reading interests, not keeping on with the strenuous reading until the fatigue point, but deliberately laying it down after the time allotted to it, and taking up a lighter subject, *with pleasure-reading in* belles-lettres *for fatigued hours.* In this way, too, he secured the same mind-set every day at the same hours.

It is amusing that with all the other sharp contrasts between Thomas Jefferson and Alexander Hamilton, they seem also to have differed fundamentally as readers and students; not in the love of books, precisely, but in the manner of using them. Hamilton burned the midnight oil over them as well as Jefferson. Hamilton also kept his reading habits in active life. He read with a restless, lashing energy, walking the floor. He read intensively. We may be sure that he tore the heart out of a book with enormous speed. He wanted the latest books from the London stalls whether, at the moment, they fitted his aim exactly, or not. He did not sit down to his reading massively, quietly, patiently. He could have walked the continent with the restless energy he wasted pacing up and down devouring his books. He could not possibly have entered the arena with Jefferson except in political science.

f) Alexander Hamilton — The restless fast reader

The story of Abraham Lincoln's educating himself on a shovel has become a part of the American epic. Like Franklin, he begged or borrowed every book in sight. Very pleasant is the story of his stepmother's insistence on quiet in the house for Abraham to read. At best there was very little chance for him to achieve any cosmopolitan range. The important thing for us to notice here is the way he used his self-taught reading habits in a career not only of strenuous action, but of constant, harrowing anxiety. The outlines of the life of the great war President with peace ideals are familiar in story, in drama, in popular tradition. They will not be complete until we add the picture of his reading Shakespeare's *Richard II* aloud to his family in the White House. In the midst of those sad, turbulent days he could turn to the literature he knew for refreshment in fatigued hours.

g) **Abraham Lincoln — The patient reader**

Perhaps if we were asked to pick out the American standing especially for action in the world of affairs we should all agree in naming Theodore Roosevelt, who passed his phrase, "The Strenuous Life," into American history. Yet that man not only published twenty-six books of his own, but was a tireless reviewer of other books, and a rapid reader. He was a sort of colonel of rough riders in reading. The amount that he covered would literally be incredible, if he had not left us some valuable hints as

h) **Theodore Roosevelt — The strenuous reader**

33

to his methods of covering the ground. Of these we shall speak presently. Let us consider first something of the man's range.

Roosevelt was Police Commissioner, Governor, Colonel, Assistant-Secretary of the Navy, Vice-President, and President of the United States in the course of his active life. Often his work day extended well into the evening. He would plunge into his reading or writing in the late hours of the day, doubtless finding change and rest in this way although he drove himself to some book always. Perhaps it was a review to be written for the *Outlook*. Many volumes in different fields were covered for review, notably in science and history. Such books as Henry Fairfield Osborn's *Origin and Evolution of Life*, Breasted's *Ancient Times*, Curtin's *Mongols*, Kidd's *Social Evolution*, Brooks Adams's *Law of Civilization and Decay*, the histories of Weigall, and many others were reviewed with considerable attention to detail. In fact Roosevelt's readings in history, — ancient, European and American, — are impressive. Herodotus, Thucydides, Polybius, Tacitus, Gibbon, Macaulay, Carlyle, Burke, Napier, Trevelyan, Motley, Parkman, even histories of De Ruyter and the merchants of the Hansa were at his finger tips. Herbert Spencer was an old acquaintance. In politics and

Roosevelt's range in reading

34

economics he was at home with authorities like Adam Smith, Malthus, Lord Aeton, Bagehot, Turgot. He enjoyed naturalists like Stewart Edward White and Hudson. John Burroughs was a family friend in the cabin at Pine Knot, near Washington. Roosevelt knew Thoreau's books. We find a rather surprising interest in poetry. Milton, Goethe, Keats, Gray, the Greek tragedies, ancient Irish sagas, the Heims Kringla, the Saga of Burnt Njal appealed to him in various ways. He read the books of liberal progressives like Croly and Weyl. And fiction? He read *Anna Karenina* when camping on the Little Missouri. He refers to Smollett, Scott, Jane Austen, Thackeray, Dickens, Trollope, Cooper, Mark Twain, Holmes, as familiar old friends. He took the whole Pigskin Library with him to the African jungle. He devoured books so voraciously that he himself said that it would be hopeless to enumerate even all the kinds of books he read. The Syracuse Public Library has put out a little pamphlet called *Roosevelt, Lover of Books*. The hunter, the politician, the writer, the President, treasured his library like any bookworm, although his reading represents only spare moments.

Here and there we have glimpses of Roosevelt's reading habits, indicated only in passing. He never tells us in so many words just how fast he reads any

35

book, nor how his rates differ in different sorts of
books, but we know that on the whole he must have
Roose- been almost incredibly rapid, even when
velt's reading difficult books. We can easily infer
methods that he sometimes skipped, and on this
point we have a delightful series of letters to his son
Kermit, about reading Dickens. Kermit had called
one of Dickens's characters maudlin. Roosevelt
agrees with Kermit, and adds: "It always interests
me about Dickens to think how much first-class work
he did, and how almost all of it was mixed up with
every kind of cheap, second-rate matter. . . . The
wise thing to do is simply to skip the bosh and twad-
dle and vulgarity and untruth, and get the benefit
out of the rest." Yet Dickens was a household word
in the Roosevelt family. Roosevelt himself is constantly referring to Dickens. The novels were well
known to him. Therefore this advice to skip comes
from a lover of Dickens. A wise, discriminating
lover, who could treasure the best, and who never
hesitated to *read over and over again Our Mutual
Friend* and *Pickwick*. Re-reading by Roosevelt is a
striking tribute not only to his interest in literature,
but to the fact that he never made speed his main
object. Roosevelt has given us in fact a list of
novels which he re-read not only once, but "over
and over-again."

36

Here it is :

Guy Mannering	*Vanity Fair*
The Antiquary	*Our Mutual Friend*
Pendennis	*Pickwick*

Roosevelt has also told us that he learned to judge the contents of a book from the index or the table of contents or the chapter headings. These would indicate to the practised reader what the subject matter includes, especially with a glance at the opening and closing sentences of the paragraphs, in the turning of the pages. "Reading with the fingers" this is called. An expert reader can do it. The most important thing to notice about Roosevelt's reading, however, is not his enormous range, so much as his free use of a whole gamut of methods for different purposes. Here in these slight hints we can see very clearly that he could finger a book, or read parts of it, skipping boldly all other parts, or read it all at a prodigious rate of speed, or read carefully for review, or read lovingly over and over again.

We could multiply instances. There is the especially interesting case of Mr. J. Ramsay MacDonald, Labor Premier of Great Britain, always occupied with political affairs, yet a reader and lover of books, almost self-taught. Whether in the country or in London Mr. MacDonald has the ever-present

i) J. Ramsay MacDonald and others

37

book in his pocket, ready to whip out if his train is late. Every corner of his library is so stuffed with books, that the weight of the shelves in his study recently endangered the floors. Sometimes a man of affairs becomes so involved that he has to use other men to read with. Mr. Lloyd George had four or five finely trained young research readers working for him in the troubled times after the armistice. Woodrow Wilson used the same method, although he was himself a trained scholar.

In general, we might perhaps say that the man of affairs tends to make use of literature rather than to become absorbed in it. Yet this is only very roughly true. The use of novels for relaxation is very clear in them all. One of the well-known surgeons of the country, on entering a serious consultation, was seen to mark very carefully his place in a detective thriller before he went in.

The late Dr. William Rainey Harper, President of the University of Chicago, trained himself to take

Decreasing speed as important as increasing it even his academic and philosophical reading at the devouring speed of a page in every sweep of his eyes, *until he came to the new and vital contribution of his author.* Here he slowed down, perhaps paused. This decrease of speed is obviously just as important as the high rate of speeding over the easy highways

of familiar ground; indeed, possibly more important, just as nothing more surely indicates good driving than the quick, practised change at the wheel
on rocky passages of road. The reader who takes
everything at racing pace never has any sure memories, nor discriminating judgments. The art lies in
knowing when and where. Edgar Allan Poe called
this art creative reading, and it is not strange to find
that his literary criticism, always too little appreciated, included in his *Essay on Reading* a statement
of the values of rapid reading for the high points of
thought. He remarked also, with that disdain for
the schools which often characterizes men of letters,
that perhaps in several generations more, children
would be taught this art of creative reading!

Meantime we need not be discouraged by these
examples of high speed and great attainment. It
should be inspiriting to realize what can be
done, and what has been done. We may **We should not be discouraged but stimulated by these examples**
not reach these peaks, but we shall climb
higher than we could without knowing
them. If a man eminent in the educational world says of his reading habits, "I
take a novel or a play at a single sitting, in
order not to break the total impression, or the con-
tinuity of thought", we may not be able to use
exactly that habit profitably, but we shall take it into

39

consideration as a valuable example of swift concentration. A well-known lawyer takes several novels an evening at times, or packs his suitcase with them for a week-end. He probably skips a great deal, but he fills in the gaps so well with his previous knowledge of the characters, with his imagination, and perhaps a glance at the chapter headings or a page now and then, that he not only knows where he is in the story, but could probably give the ordinary reader many keen observations. The story goes that Henry Ward Beecher was lunching with a friend who happened to have a book with him. In the interval of the luncheon Beecher fingered it almost absently with a glance at the pages now and then. When they had finished, his friend offered to lend him the book. With courteous thanks, Beecher said he had already finished it. Of course, what he really meant was that he had been able to judge of its contents, and perhaps could have reproduced them. He was familiar with all the approaches to the subject. Does not this fact make the achievement less discouraging? We can be sure that just so far as we master a subject, we shall read more quickly, understandingly, appraisingly, in it. It will cheer us on to know of the brilliant readers who have learned to sweep the page for new material, to concentrate rapidly upon it, to pass over familiar ground, to build between gaps, to span whole chapters with a swing like a suspension bridge, to infer whole sections from a certain sort of beginning, in short to read with constant, constructive imagination, rather than with literal, word-for-word fidelity.   On the other hand, is it not still more pleasing to have their illustrious authority for browsing over our old favorites ?   For re-reading at times ?   And for making *belles-lettres* our relaxation ?

Let us turn now to see a little more definitely how and why and where it can all be done.

CHAPTER II

WHY READ NOVELS?

GENERAL AND SPECIFIC OBJECTIVES
IN APPROACHING FICTION,
COMPARED WITH THOSE APPLYING TO
OTHER FORMS OF LITERATURE

We have seen that the reader of achievement and distinction has a tendency to unusual range and speed, with varieties of approach, unconsciously attained. There is little evidence of any deliberate plan or technique covering these varieties of approach. We have to judge by the merest scattered hints here and there. A writer tells us what he rereads with loving care, just because he wants us to understand his appreciations, the things which have made him what he is, not at all because he wishes to tell us how slowly he read. Or, again, he mentions taking a novel at a sitting, not to prove to us that it is a good thing to do, or that he has attained great speed, but because he wishes to indicate that the book was interesting

Prominence and variety of objectives on the part of distinguished readers

42

enough to hold him to the spot. Now and then we find a hint such as Roosevelt's about the free use of indexes and tables of contents, with chapter headings. By piecing together such scattering bits of technique we know that readers of long practice can judge very quickly the quality and method of a particular book, can seize its essential contribution, particularly its *new* contribution, can concentrate rapidly upon it, knowing just when and where, how and how much to read slowly or even re-read, when and where, how and how much to skim at an enormous rate, and how much to skip altogether. We have seen that they can read while they talk, while they walk, while they travel, and even while they work at something else. We have seen great variety in suiting their methods to their purposes in reading.

This coincides directly with one of the most fundamental principles of modern education, — namely, that methods should everywhere be governed first of all by definite objectives, instead of by flat, unchanging standards of accomplishment or knowledge. The field of human knowledge has broadened to such an extent that we can approach it only in certain definite aspects, parts, or divisions, for certain definite objectives. Therefore it is significant and helpful to notice this wide variety of reading adapted to changing, flexible purposes, even though these distinguished readers can give us little help in working out the full and exact technique of approach which we are demanding in all subjects today.

Before we come to any discussion of technique, therefore, we must first ask ourselves what the objectives of our approach are. Why read novels at all? Does the general approach to a novel differ enough from that to a play, a poem, an essay, a history, or a biography, to need its own special technique? Or, are the objectives and therefore the principles governing us in taking up a novel merely the general objectives and principles of reading? If novels should be read with very special ends in view how shall we determine these?

What are the objectives of novel-reading?

When we think of our week-end holiday reading, what is the first suggestion that appeals to us? A play? A poem? An essay? A biography? A history? All the popular week-end lists would favor novels, although a biography or a history might be thrown in as well. Novels hold our attention most easily, on the whole, with a rapid, crescendo interest in the narrative, in the interplay of characters, in the definite conclusion. As a rule, we can lose ourselves more fully at once in the novel than in any other form of literature.

General Objectives. I. Relaxation. Reading for the Narrative

44

There may be many individual exceptions to this rule, but in general the fact will not be denied. Here is our first general objective in reading novels. An age-old relaxation in emotional escape. The outlet for strain, fatigue, and worry, through a novel in which we can lose ourselves and yet find ourselves in the experiences we share, is recognized as wholesome the world over. Our first chapter has shown how readers of distinction have turned to novels for relaxation. Thackeray, in the first number of his *Roundabout Papers*, after telling us that he has himself read his Dumas "for thirteen hours of a happy day", when ill in bed, goes on to tell us how many clever, hard-headed men like novel-reading; how many physicians, judges, bishops, chancellors, mathematicians are notorious novel-readers; how the appetite for novels extends to the end of the world, "far away in the frozen deep, the sailors reading them to one another during the endless night; far away under the Syrian stars, the solemn Sheikhs and Elders hearkening to the poet as he recites his tales; far away in the Indian camps, where the soldiers listen. . . ."

It is a form of relaxation which cannot be replaced by the base-ball score or the movie-film or the spoken drama, although these latter have their own place. Our restless Western habits need quieting

pleasures, need relief from strain at times when no
theatre will do as well, when perhaps fatigue en-
forces rest. Then what a resource the novel becomes, the novel that keeps us from tossing on our
own problems, and getting further away from solution as we toss! He who has not learned this
resource misses a vital help in the complex strains
of modern life, for the greatest rest comes in a
change of thought, not in vacancy. We should *use*
our novel-reading for fatigue and strain. Is there
anyone who cannot recall taking journeys, in which
the attempt to read left at first only meaningless
signs dancing on the page, but after a time brought
intelligence and something like calmness? A novel
in one's hand, one can turn the rocking roar of the
subway train or the jerking commuter's local into a
genuine relaxation. One need never glare at the
clock in any delay, nor keep on reading the fastest
growing cigarette advertisement, nor stare vacantly
at fellow-passengers about whom we have already
noted all the details. There need be no flat stretches
of road, no dull country house, no tedious voyage.

A second objective often expressed by novel-
readers, past and present, is the rich knowledge of
human life, and the surroundings of human life,
which novels can impart in a fuller way than any
other form of literature. Many of them are, in

truth, excellent studies in social psychology. The social types of character in any particular district of the earth have never been so completely and so realistically set forth as in novels. Just as a matter of knowledge of our fellows and of ordinary understanding of life outside our own circles, we cannot afford to be ignorant of Arnold Bennett's novels of the pottery districts of England, of Ladislas Reymont's studies of Polish peasants, of Dostoiefsky's Russian village types, of the intensely French life in Balzac, Daudet, Rolland, Flaubert, of the Italian characters of Fogazzaro; or of the American Main Streets, Babbitts, and Arrowsmiths. There would probably be no hesitation among any judges of Mr. Sinclair Lewis's novels as works of art, if they were to be compared with Susan Glaspell's one-act play, *Trifles*, or Robert Frost's poem, *The Death of the Hired Man*, or Edwin Arlington Robinson's *Isaac and Archibald*, or Carl Sandburg's *Nocturne in a Deserted Brickyard* or *Fog*. Mr. Lewis's novels could not hold their own against any of these as works of art. But if a foreigner wished to know of life in different aspects in the United States he would be sent to these novels, and the poems would scarcely be thought of, while the fine little one-act tragedy,

Marginal note: II. Second general objective a richer knowledge of life and environment.

a) Larger social wholes

47

Trifles, could be of only the most general suggestiveness. The objective in reading would make all the difference. Novels can, of course, be highly evolved works of art, but our main or first objective in reading them is seldom æsthetic.

This use of novels for sociological purposes extends to the novels of the past as well as to the present. Volumes of eighteenth-century or early nineteenth-century novels will be found on reference shelves in history or sociology courses, to an increasing degree. The case for novel-reading from this point of view has been vividly put by Mr. St. John Ervine, playwright and novelist, in his novel, *Changing Winds*, from which we quote a racy bit scoring social workers who do not make use of novels as their great sources for knowledge of life:

"No wonder, he thought to himself, all reformers and serious people make such a mess of the social system when they despise and ignore the principal means of knowing the human spirit (*i.e.* literature).

"'That's a pity,' he said aloud, 'I should have thought that you'd find novels useful to you in your work. I mean, there's surely more chance of understanding the people of the eighteenth century if you read Fielding's *Tom Jones*, than there is if you read Lecky's *England in the Eighteenth Century*.

"'Is there?' said Rachel. 'Of course there is,' Gilbert hurled at her from the other side of the table. 'Fielding was an artist, inspired by God, but Lecky was simply a fact-pedlar, inspired by the Board of Education. Why, even that dull ass, Richardson, makes you understand more about his period than Lecky does.'"

Novels as social studies in the broadly human sense may need much solid reading of the fact-pedlars to accompany them, if we are to have any exact data. Novels do not give reports, summaries, tables, percentages, correlations, nor averages. All these are necessary, but they are quite outside the scope of the novel. A novel may even give a thoroughly prejudiced emotional slant on a public question, past or present. No one in his senses would make up a prison report from *Little Dorrit*, or discuss seriously the educational methods of Squeers, or the business ventures of Micawber, or the law tangles of Mr. Jarndyce and Mr. Bumble. Nevertheless, he who has never felt the Marshalsea prison with Dickens, who has never shared his noble hate for Dotheboys Hall, or the English workhouse of his day, who has never waited with Micawber for something to turn up, who has never said with Bumble "the law is a ass", is very seriously handicapped in a full human understanding of Dickens's England, since Dickens is ever a first-hand source of human feeling about it, actually causing changes in it to an appreciable extent. Probably we never quite fully realize how largely the dynamic power in social change is emotional. The record of these origins in feeling often exists in novels.

It is not only in the understanding of past and present movements in society that the novel can broaden our views. It can also transport us to foreign countries, without a passport or a letter of credit. In this sense it becomes "vicarious travel", to use the happy expression of Dr. William Bagley. The casual traveller would not see all that a good foreign novel gives him. It could probably be demonstrated that an understanding reading of the four volumes of Ladislas Reymont's *Peasants* would be in many respects better than a visit to Poland, certainly than a casual visit to Poland. It takes years of patient, intimate knowledge of Polish village life to build such a novel. Here is a consoling fact for the person who cannot travel. Those of us who have ever had the experience of hearing returned travellers say to us, "I didn't know before that you had been there", when as a matter of fact we have not, will appreciate the truth of the argument.

So far we have been speaking of novels as sociological material, dealing with the broader social aspects of time and place.   When we come to studies in personality, as they abound in novels, we are on even surer ground.   Three hundred years ago Cervantes painted an introvert and an extrovert wandering through the plain of La Mancha, in Spain.   He had never heard of these epithets for his characters. But his analysis is expert, deserving careful study, as well as appreciation.   Knowledge of the more baffling motives and conflicts in human nature has been common in the masters of fiction, sometimes hundreds of years before the psychologists could attack them.   Novels, by their very nature, can give more space to the analysis of these problems than other forms of literature.   We have, therefore, a mine of study almost unworked.   Madame Bovary can show us what may happen to a rich imagination, stifled in a provincial town.   Eugénie Grandet, a peasant of the higher order, suffers more quietly and submissively, until her bleached and deadened emotions are like a blank white wall.   Turgenev can delineate, with exquisite detail, the poignant, subtle tragedies in the relations between parents and children.   Galsworthy can carry us through a long, complex strain between husband and wife.   Among the characters in our own recent American novels,

b) Novels can give us a richer understanding of personality and personal adjustment

we have seen Porgy, the old negro beggar, analyzed with amazing vividness, and the old bachelor beau of a commonplace family traced down to the very roots of his emotional failure. If it is true that successful living depends very largely on the delicate personal adjustments we make, then we cannot have too many examples of varied types before us. A well-known European psychiatrist has said that Dostoiefsky's pathological characters are authoritative cases worthy of study. They are, however, easier for the ordinary person to understand than case-studies, phrased in technical terms. The imagination of the novelist penetrates them, takes the human reality and puts it before us. We shall find our thinking enriched with a whole gallery of forceful examples in adjustment and maladjustment. Nor does it especially concern us in this connection if the personal portraits in novels are not exact, scientific case-studies in all respects. We never take them for such, as we read. They serve their purpose if they suggest possibilities to us, and widen the horizons of our imaginative sympathies. The very fact that we begin to compare the characters in a novel with persons we know, or have known, shows that we are stimulated.

In addition to the general objectives, we shall need to recognize many specific objectives, differing greatly with the individual. There is the æsthetic approach, not so commonly used in reading novels as in appreciating other forms of art, yet valuable and highly important. There is the student's interest in the historical novel, a somewhat doubtful, hybrid form, useful to convey the spirit of a period in historical study. There is the antiquarian interest in reading many quaint novels of the past. Very important, also, are certain definite, specific training objectives for teachers and students of reading to consider. *Need of more specific objectives*

In these training objectives we are on the ground made familiar by the work of experts, who have shown us that reading is not one type of skill, but many. These skills, or special abilities in reading, require special train- ing. In other words, reading is a highly complex matter, involving not only mastery of complicated techniques, but the ability to choose which technique is best suited to a particular purpose. We must have, not only complete control of our reading skills, but the judgment to turn them off and on at will, so to speak. We must have variety in handling, judging, adapting the material claiming our eyes so constantly. Certainly there are objectives that call for speed, and others that call for slow reading. *Specific training objectives*

53

The old-fashioned reading lesson held everything on one level. The simplest facts were read aloud in a dawdling, wasteful way, while the brightest pupils either lost interest or went ahead by peeping or guessing. The slowest never had any training in casting the eye ahead of the voice to gain a wide perceptual span of many words in one sweep, or a wide eye-voice span, *i.e.*, the difference between the exact point of articulation and the point of the eye-fixation. This eye-fixation should be in all rapid silent reading ahead of any point that could be reached by the voice at any particular instant. Training in silent reading reduces the number of eye-fixations or pauses which the eyes necessarily make at various points in their journey across the printed line. The fewer the pauses the greater the speed. The more the eyes take in before they pause, the wider the span of recognition, the more unimpeded and smooth the progress down the page. Along with this training goes the suppression of vocalization. Although experiment has shown that the vocal cords of even a practised reader make slight movements corresponding to the word, speed and efficiency may be obtained in silent reading only by the suppression of pronounced inner speech, vocal activities, motor and auditory associations. No whispering of the words! No pointing with pencil

54

or finger! These are sure marks of a poor silent reader. Recognition should be instant from print to meaning, without even stopping for form, much less for sound.

Such practised reading would be a difficult and complex art in itself, but it is not all. Do we never need the precise vocalization which we suppress? Do we never need to submit the words to inward hearing? Or reading aloud? Or listening? Or frankly pausing? Assuredly we do. There are objectives that call for slow reading. Here lies the delicate problem of judgment for every reader. It cannot be settled off-hand. That we need oral reading, or at least inward speech, will be manifest at once when we consider *Paradise Lost*, or *The Odyssey*, or Keats's *Ode to a Nightingale*. No one has ever appreciated these by silent rapid reading methods. They must be *heard*. This is almost equally true of passages in Dickens, Scott, Thackeray, and other novelists. What we need, evidently, is a long, graduated range of power in reading, from the fastest scanning for easy material of no particular beauty, to slow reading aloud for the literature that should be heard and shared.

Now it happens that novels afford greater practice in all these rates and varieties of speed than any other form of literature. They offer this practice in a very intensified way, and, unlike much valuable training, they offer it painlessly. From the time of

Extent to which novels call for different rates of reading

the third grade, when the eye-voice span begins to widen, the adventure story will accelerate the silent-reading process to a marked degree. For the objectives of silent reading are exactly the natural reading objectives in approaching the end of a thrilling story. It is not necessary to tell the child who is in the grip of *Treasure Island*, or *Kidnapped*, or *The Pathfinder*, to read sentence groups rather than individual words, to leap from one sentence to the next, not dwelling on the words, to let two or three salient words stand for the rest, and not pause to hear the words, nor submit them in any way to inward hearing. What does he care whether the word be "stormy" or "tempestuous", "bright" or "shining", "slay" or "kill"? He wants to know how it all comes out, and can safely be trusted to know even better than the author which parts are most relevant to that end. He will begin to sift values, choose, and skip without knowing it. He will hardly see the individual words, in his haste. He is acquiring a valuable skill, with a natural incentive.

This is only the beginning of novel-reading practice. There are the stories that provoke questions even in young readers. Did all the queer things in

The House of the Seven Gables happen, or are they just creepy suggestions ? Did *The Snow Image* really jump about in the cold north wind ? Children will ask these questions themselves, and questions mean a slower rate. Problems of character and thought, of style and action, grow naturally more complex in a child's novel-reading until by slow degrees he reaches a reflective reading not unlike study. Passages demanding dramatic oral presentation for their full appreciation will occur more frequently. Last of all, probably, he may wish to re-read some passages for their marked beauty of style, and make a study of their art. All these procedures of reading technique will be considered in detail in later chapters. The point to be noted at present is that novel-reading can give us the widest possible control of our own techniques.

Why novels require different rates of reading. Explanation afforded by history and form of the novel

Why is this control more varied than that in reading poetry, drama, essays, or history ? A glance at the history of the novel-form will show that the novel of contemporary life and manners was evolved in the early eighteenth century out of many varieties of literature. The romance of an earlier day contributed its quota, and has always remained more or less a part of the novel. This gives us the adventure, the plot, the hair-breadth escapes, the heavy villains. In the early eighteenth century the current forms of interest were the essay, the letter, the character-sketch, the presentation of contemporary manners. These combined with the earlier story-material to make a new form of very bulky proportions and composite character. Fielding stops his story at any time to intersperse a satirical essay, or poke fun in other ways at contemporary life, without any regard to the plot. Richardson went to about 200,000 words in *Clarissa Harlowe*. Dickens reached almost that figure in many of his novels. There is nothing concrete to stop a novelist from this uninterrupted flow of his own thought. He can sit in his study and imagine his gentle reader following every turn. The form in which he is writing is so flexible with accretions from other sources that he can slip in biography, autobiography, speculation, satire, philosophy, religion, antiquarian details, reminiscences, ethics, and, of late years, all the sciences and pseudo-sciences.

Imagine an audience sitting through a Scott or a Thackeray introduction at the theatre! There would be a rush in the lobby before the genealogy had reached Henry Esmond or Colonel Newcome. The dramatist even in his freest periods has to consider fixed limits.

Drama and novel contrasted as reading

Consequently the form of drama is more compressed, condensed, and suggestive. After all, we make our own Hamlet. We must think, always, through the necessary gaps in the dramatist's form. He sketches for us. He suggests to us. Hence the reading rate in drama cannot be, as a rule, much faster than the spoken form, and it is more or less a constant, instead of a variable. Poetry should be heard by the inward ear if not by the outward. This fact also makes for a more constant, slower rate. Essays, history, science, all mean closer thinking, and usually will require a more even rate of reading.

We do not make our own David Copperfield. He is made for us in 900 pages or so. Lovers of Dickens do not find this too long, and the matter at issue is not at all the matter of merit, but only the natural difference in approach. We have a right to treat our novelist more cavalierly, more familiarly, to pick and choose more easily, to say to him now and then : "Friend, you are repeating yourself", or "You're off the subject, old dear." For he probably will both repeat and wander. It is only in the rare emanation of an artist, like Flaubert or Turgenev, that we find the novel to be read quite through with an even, unchanging rate, and without the loss of a single word. In reading most novels we can vary and

59

choose perhaps eight or ten different rates, methods, attitudes, as we shall see more in detail in later chapters.

With such a control of our technique in reading, it would be possible to cover the major part of the season's output of novels every year. Some critics may contest the desirability of doing so. If we include this as an objective in any sense, however, it will be with the knowledge that we shall probably not often be reading permanent literature. Emerson's advice never to read any book until it is at least a year old had in view the sifting of solid values of lasting worth. Time will do this sifting for us if we are incompetent to do it for ourselves. Aside from the fact that on this plan we should have missed *Pickwick* when he came fresh from his author's pen, does it not also mean a further loss? Shall we not be losing one valuable source of lively, quick understanding of our own time, at this very moment of its changing course? Is not such understanding an important help against growing old and stale? By all means let us keep our old friends in literature, and re-read them as often as we like! But if we find ourselves reading *only* old novels, let us beware! The clock is striking.

Influence of these objectives on our reading of current novels. Shall we cover the season's output?

It may very naturally be objected that reading a large number of the novels of a season would be impossible even for a reviewer, especially if he tried to do justice to foreign fiction as well as to English and American. The ideal here is not by any means to read it all, but rather to cover it all, to survey it all, to know all the types of fiction in the market, to be able to judge these from hints, selections, reviews, and finally to select our own. The sooner we acquire the habit of scanning reviews, the better. We should plan to read a score or more every week, in journals as widely varied as possible. Practice will soon make one skilled in allowing for the point of view, or possibly bias, of the reviewer of the journal at hand. By comparing various reviews, one can reach very shortly some idea of the type of novel being reviewed, and its general mode of treatment, its main characters, and its moot questions or problems. This sort of review-scanning need not take much time. It will afford excellent practice in getting values swiftly, since the reviewer himself, unless of unusual worth, need not detain us. It will not matter if we lose a sentence or two, as we cast our eyes down his column for hints about a new novel. But our reading of reviews will be almost useless if we do not take the

Influence on our reading of reviews. How to use the reviews of novels intelligently

pains to accompany it with a note-book for jotting down a note or two about the books which seem most significant, or most likely to meet our own personal objectives. If we do this, we shall have a ready list, always at hand, for the next week-end trip, or the next tedious journey, or the next evening which finds us too fatigued for other things. We shall not have to ransack our memories for the best novels to take, and perhaps end in picking up something by chance. We shall know what we want, and why, and our reading will take on purpose. We shall find ourselves in command of the best fiction of the hour almost without noticing the steps by which we have done it.

Readers may ask which reviews will best lead to these wide objectives. It seems a good thing to begin very naturally with one's Sunday **What reviews shall we read?** Book Review Supplement. The inhabitant of Manhattan thinks with ready, New York provincialism of his *Times*, or his *Herald Tribune*, or his *Post*. The point may well be left to individual preference, since it is only the beginning. One should pass on directly to the weekly reviews, like Mr. Henry Seidel Canby's *Saturday Review*, *The New Republic*, *The Living Age*, *The Nation*, and the London weekly, *The Spectator*, if possible. The monthlies will come next. Here

62

The Bookman and *The International Book Review* will admirably offset *The American Mercury*. If we are to have any range in our aims, it is almost a necessity to read English reviews such as the excellent *London Mercury*, edited by J. C. Squire, and *The Contemporary Review*. Also, it is not asking too much even of a nation of lazy linguists to make ourselves familiar with the well-known French reviews, *Mercure de France*, *La Revue des Deux Mondes*, *La Nouvelle Revue*, *L'Illustration*, *La Nouvelle Revue Française*. Remember that European fiction is known, reviewed, and translated in France often several years before it is known to any extent here. If we are to develop cosmopolitan culture on this continent, we shall have to develop first the cosmopolitan mind. Fiction gives most fully the typical ways of thinking and of living in a nation. Should we not get them at the earliest possible moment? It seems increasingly certain that a greater understanding among peoples would grow out of a more immediate interchange of literature, especially of fiction.

One major objective already implied is the rapid seizure of the author's main idea or purpose. What sort of thing is this writer before us attempting to do? Does he wish to flay abuses? Does he wish to give us a light, cynical story? Is his interest rather in conveying unusual types of character? Is he interested in subtle phases of individual and

Seizing the author's purpose. Relation of the author's purpose to the reader's social psychology, or in racial traits such as *A Passage to India* shows? Is it painstaking local color that he wishes to give us? Is it a good story, merely? Whatever the main purpose, we must seize it early, on first opening the book, if possible, and guide our technique in reading by the author's main objective. Later chapters will give more detailed analysis of these points.

The author's purpose, then, will be a guide. But it may not be the main objective for the reader.

Seizing one's own purpose That can never be anything but *one's own purpose*, if reading is to be most fruitful. What are *we* reading for? What does the reader expect to get out of it? To know what we want in the merest good story adds zest to the whole thing. But it does far more than this. A much more important factor in the present discussion is the modification of our reading habits by our purposes at the time. The flexible use of our techniques will be of very little profit if we turn them on at the wrong object, at the wrong time.

Take, for instance, *The House of the Seven Gables*. Hawthorne's main objective lies in the symbolic art of the story, as he plays his symbols in and out of

64

life, producing finally an elaborate pattern of highly sophisticated art. Young readers will hardly touch this objective, except little by little, as they are guided to it. Their purpose will be the story. They will read with a fairly smooth, even pace, and no very particular emphasis on minute details. These very details will be important to the *Illustration in reading. The House of the Seven Gables* student of literature. He will read far more slowly, noting the perfection of art by which Hawthorne accumulates his creepy suggestions and symbols to express his main idea over and over again. The student of literary art, in other words, has the same objective that Hawthorne himself had. But suppose one is studying the development of persecution phases in Puritan pathology. The Pyncheons and the Maules, though fanciful, will be admirable portraits to study. With such an aim, the student of psychology will neglect many picturesque descriptive details, and concentrate his reading on the analysis of states of Pyncheon and Maule minds, — an analysis which Hawthorne himself took a great deal of pains to give. Or again, suppose one is studying Puritan life for a history problem. One would then concentrate on events and surroundings, the environmental interests in the story. Such an objective would be clearer still if one were intending to write

65

a paper on old Salem, or the witchcraft cases in particular. One would then neglect everything *but* the very details of town life which we neglected before. From one point of view it is a pity to use a piece of literary art for other purposes than that for which it was made. Yet Hawthorne knew his Salem with imaginative depth, from wide reading in its past, and from long, sensitive contemporary contacts. Is it not perfectly legitimate to use his knowledge and experience and imagination, wherever they will be useful? Provided especially that in pursuing any aim of our own, we do not forget that *The House of the Seven Gables* is first of all art.

Hawthorne's *Marble Faun* also can be approached in different ways. Ordinarily, one would read with

Other illustrations of adapting reading skills to one's purpose Hawthorne's own purpose, — to seize the art of the situation, with its contrasting figures, its high lights and deep shadows, and its haunting mystery, set against the baffling power of Rome. Suppose one is going to Italy for the first time. The very fact that Hawthorne has given his own first impressions imparts a naïve, æsthetic quality to the book. He stops to describe not only his marble faun in the Capitoline museum, but the view down the steps of the arch of Septimius Severus, the Forum, the Coliseum, the Alban hills, and the Etrus-

66

can, Roman, and Christian ruins everywhere. Later in the story he gives a full description of Perugia, with Pisano's sculptured fountain in the market place, and the statue of Pope Julius III beyond, near the cathedral. The little Umbrian villages perched on crags of rock are all indicated as they appear to the eyes of the sensitive American. The faded roadside shrines appealed to him. He lingered over Donatello's tower in the Apennines, where an Italian novelist would probably give it a word or so. Is it strange that *The Marble Faun* has been used as a guide book by Americans ? We linger quite properly over all these passages if we wish to absorb something of the spirit of Italy before going there. But if an Italian reader were interested in the book, he would as readily pass over these details to the contrasts of character, and the symbolic art of the story. Similarly, if a reader were especially interested in antiquities of Scotland, he would read much more slowly certain parts of Scott's novels than he otherwise naturally would. These suggestions as to rate and attitude will be treated in later chapters. The point to be noted here is the main objective of seizing one's own purpose first, in order to decide *how* to read, or what particular skill best suits this purpose.

Let us now turn to more specific aids in reading novels.

CHAPTER III

TESTS AND OTHER GENERAL AIDS
IN NOVEL-READING

For the past twelve years we have offered an undergraduate course including the study of the novel at Teachers College, Columbia University. **Observations in Teachers College, Columbia University** The number of students enrolled each year has been approximately three hundred. We have therefore met between 3500 and 3600 students in this course, a large, homogeneous college group for observation and record. We began with the ordinary, flat, wholesale assignments, course readings, bibliographies, and all the paraphernalia derived more or less from the academic college tradition. Radical changes have been necessary in the light of actual needs, and of real objectives.

We have found that piling up questions, topics, problems, study material, does not help the reading process itself. These topics all refer to the "what" of the text, the understanding of its matter, never the "how", the manner of attacking it. For example, I have before me a published series of admirable questions and suggestions supposedly to help the study of Poe's *Cask of Amontillado, The Fall of the House of Usher, The Gold Bug*, and *The Purloined Letter*. There are explanations of the text, cross references, biographical and bibliographical data, discussions of literary technique, problems of meaning, and in fact everything that could elucidate the *what* of the text, but never the first hint as to *how* to attack it. There is not even a suggestion that *The Purloined Letter* can be read with the speed appropriate to a detective thriller, while *The Fall of the House of Usher* will need reflective pauses now and then for its artistic details and its symbolic treatment. Here is a fine opportunity to show our student reader the difference between the values of swift, silent reading and slow reflective reading, with the pauses indicated, etc. And it is an opportunity completely lost.

How have our students been helped?

Students who come to us after years of preparatory and even professional experience have no idea whatever of such differences. The pages of their books lie before them like a flat, white plain, to be covered in steady marches, with no inspiriting gallops between.

Our first measure of help, then, lay in breaking up these forced marches, so often a matter of conscience

69

to the faithful student. We seemed to be violating his ideas of thoroughness. The various tests in use,

A new attitude towards reading with all their immense helpfulness for many purposes, do not greatly change the emphasis on careful, exact knowledge of all details in the text. The very fact that a comprehension check has to be used, with its objective standards, does not encourage rapid sifting of the text for the student's own personal aims, or subjective values. Far from it. How does he know that some apparently unimportant detail might not be considered important when the inevitable question comes? So with all such useful helps as the repression of vocalizing, the constant practice with time control, the short exposure exercises, the training in habits of regular, uniform, rhythmical eye movements, — all very useful and necessary, but not in themselves creating the attitude of bold choice and discriminating judgment in the reader. First of all he must be helped to feel that it is his own reading, for his own purpose, not necessarily matching any other person's aim at that moment, and not necessarily involving this or that fact in the book.

In short, it is nothing less than a new standard of thoroughness which is needed. Thoroughness involves neglect. The paradox expresses a sound principle. Any musician recognizes it when he ignores notes in his score because they can safely be assumed. He sees only the significant new combinations. Just so the reader should ignore many details in most books, in order to concentrate rapidly upon the important ideas new to him in his purpose at the moment. He should always hold the threads of these firmly in hand, along with the main outlines of the author's thought, to be filled in just when and where he finds it necessary and nowhere else. He must not be lost in details. Thoroughness also involves imagination, — the ability to bridge gaps, to build between the parts of an author's thought, to know what he must have said, at certain points, to infer conclusions from beginnings, to dare omissions in the economy of thought and time and also to dare the reflective pauses which are just as important, no matter how much they slow down the rate. Emerson's idea that there is creative reading as well as creative writing is exactly in line with the present distinctions. Creative reading selects constantly for further use. It is always making new connections in the subject. Sometimes it is worth while to read with a note-book at hand for jotting down impressions. Above all, thoroughness does not necessarily involve repetition, except in drill work, and certainly

A new standard of thoroughness

not in narrative fiction, where, by an amusing irony, we so often find it.

Such an ideal of thoroughness will break up any fixed pace in reading, once and for all. It will mean flexible rates, adapted to different purposes. Doubtless an improvement in speed, with its required additional concentration on the main points, is an excellent thing for the more or less familiar, easy highroads. Narrative fiction should commonly be classed here since novels are the best training-ground for facility in rapid silent reading. They afford the very life-situation for natural speed, motivated by natural interest in the story. But they do more than this, as we saw in discussing the training objectives in the last chapter. They give more chances to practise *rapid changes in rate* than any other form of literature. From a fast rate to a moderately fast rate, from a moderate rate to a slow, reflective rate, the reader can travel the scale with rapid variety in most fiction. We shall, in later chapters, definitely advise skimming and skipping; but we shall also suggest slowing down, even reading aloud, and studying, in some instances.

What becomes of a fixed reading rate?

Our students have responded with zest to the idea of enjoying a novel at a sitting, once we have released their scruples about trying to remember what hap-

pened on page 19, or what kind of fur coat the
heroine wears, or what racing car the hero drives.
The upper third or fourth of any class
gains very high reading rates after a few
weeks of practice and help, not infrequently
reaching reviewers' rates of about four
hundred and eighty words a minute. This
means skimming over the ground without
seeing the individual sentences. Yet this speed
should never be breathless. We should be fast, without hurry. No rushing. There can be a very harm-
ful superficial jumping over the lines with no sense
of their meaning. We must try to avoid this, even
in our highest rate. Of equal importance is the
flexible, quick change to a slower rate, or even a
pause at the page requiring thought. We should
never fear to re-read a sentence. The actual test
results given here show that the best readers slow
down more freely than the mediocre readers when
a difficult point is reached. *The fixed rate,
whether fast or slow, is not the ideal.*

What are some of the definite aids to
reading which we have found most helpful
with our thirty-five hundred students?
Needless to say, we have used all the
well-known helps in the repression of vocalization, the constant practice with time control,

*Helping
our stu-
dents to
break up
their fixed
reading
rates*

*Some
definite
special
aids in
reading
novels.
I. Pre-
paratory
discussion*

73

the short-exposure exercises, the training in eye-movements, etc. In addition to these devices, and quite in line with the researches of Dearborn, we have found that any previous familiarity with the subject, story, author, treatment, style, or problem makes an almost immediate increase in speed when one actually attacks the book in question. We tried this out informally many times by asking whole classes to read a book about which they had no previous ideas whatever, and then to read immediately afterwards a book of the same qualities about which they had heard some discussion, but in which they had not read a word. The results were always rapid increases of speed in the latter. This means not only that advance assignments should always be "warmed up" ahead of time by the teacher, but that students should hear all the discussion possible from one another, in, before, and after classes; should read reviews, synopses, introductions; should stimulate talk in good company everywhere; should get everybody who has read anything to talk about it.

Another decided help, based on the same principles, is the early recognition of what we may call "idea-cues" in an author, corresponding exactly to the recognition of word-cues in reading. We all know that the improvement in reading rates, in general, is due to many complex causes. The word-

74

cues (familiar letters on the page in familiar combinations) lead to the recognition of whole phrases, clauses, and sentences, in the associative complex. Precisely the same recognition of idea-cues should take place. For instance, Thackeray's idea of the evil of enforced marriages becomes very familiar. It may cover four or five pages of his novel at any time. He may develop it in essay, sermonette, anecdote, appeal, or history, but there it is. The same idea. The second, third, and fourth time it occurs, the recognition should be correspondingly rapid, until finally it should become entirely a matter of individual judgment and taste as to whether one should read completely through the passage, or skim it, or glance at the beginning and the end to make sure that there is nothing vitally new, or skip it altogether. The Thackeray lover will doubtless read straight through. He has every right to do so. But those who do not find themselves especially in need of another illustration of a long-familiar point have their rights as well.

II. Another aid. Recognizing "idea-cues"

It follows very naturally that we shall read all authors with greater economy of time and attention if we read two or three of their novels successively, when possible. We then become thoroughly familiar with the characteristic idea-cues, the points of view,

75

the interests at large of our novelist. The second and third novel will find us slipping with ease past the opening situations with no more awk- ward difficulties of introduction due to strangeness. *Old Mortality* is easier after *Waverley*, *Our Mutual Friend* is easier after *David Copperfield*, *Pendennis* is easier after *The Newcomes*, *Far from the Madding Crowd* is easier after *The Return of the Native*, and *The Ambassadors* is easier after *The American*. Such an attack has the added ad-

III. It is therefore wise to read two or three novels of the same author successively

vantage of making our novelist a distinct person, with marked individuality, as we come to know him well.

One of the most persistent difficulties which our students find is in starting a new novel. "If we could only get into it" is the constant cry. "We enjoyed it after we once passed the opening." Getting under way is in- deed the slow part of any occupation whatever. It is a well-known law of any reading or study that we have to be

IV. Why are we so often dis- couraged at the be- ginning of a novel?

"warmed up" to it like cold engines at the start. This is very natural, especially if we begin a novel with no antecedent preparation. What are all these people in it to us, anyway? We find it tedious to get up an interest in them, especially if we have to

76

follow the family tree for generations before even reaching the characters. As to the definite procedure in such cases, we shall have more to say in a later chapter. The point to note at present is that we should accept this difficulty in getting under way as not only very natural, but as in no way indicating the pace we shall take later on in the book. We have been able to save our students from discouragement by telling them that if they will be a little patient about the opening chapters, grip the situation firmly with a little effort at first, they will find themselves rewarded by a steep rise of interest and of reading rate, as they fall into the story. Then it often happens that somewhere after the middle of the book, interest and rate decline somewhat, unless the novelist has sustained his work unusually well. Here there is always room for judgment in skipping. There is, however, a rise toward the conclusion again as we hasten on to get the final solution. Of course we are indicating only in the most general way what is likely to be the line of reading-interest and rate in a novel. There can be all sorts of variations. A novel can lead us steeply to its very conclusion, without our being once willing to put it down; or it can give us its main interest in the first third, and then fall off; or it can give us a long dull stretch with a breathless

77

last third. The varieties are very great. Speaking of the average novel, we may perhaps say that the line of reading rate will be something like this:

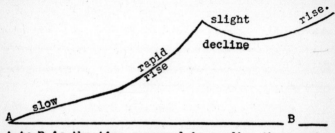

A to B is the time consumed in reading the novel.

We gave recently a series of test readings in different types of fiction, with the aid of research **Reading tests** instructors and students in psychology. We made our selections from ten different standard novelists ranging from Jane Austen to Galsworthy. So far as possible, these selections were complete units of the story, about one thousand words each, taken bodily out of the text, and mimeographed for the reading tests, with letters as the only titles. Each student was thus given copies entitled only *Selection X*, *Selection Y*, etc. Although we aimed to give rather unfamiliar passages, there was nothing of peculiar or vexing difficulty.

78

Our ten reading units or passages selected were the following:

1. Selection X. The episode from Stevenson's *Kidnapped*, in which David Balfour is sent up the ruined tower stairs by his treacherous uncle. The units selected

2. Selection Y. A passage from Hawthorne's *Scarlet Letter*, in which Hester Prynne is meditating on Puritan standards of thought and conduct.

3. Selection S. Mr. Campbell, of Scott's *Rob Roy*, is introduced to the reader.

4. Selection A. A characteristic bit of dialogue and description contrasting Eleanor and Marianna from Jane Austen's *Sense and Sensibility*.

5. Selection D. An episode between Pip and Miss Havisham from Dickens's *Great Expectations*.

6. Selection G. Mr. Stone reads a portion of his book to Bianca and Hilary in Galsworthy's *Fraternity*.

7. Selection T. Thackeray's description of Mr. Warrington's theatre-party in *The Virginians*.

8. Selection J. A passage from Henry James's *Ambassadors*, in which the atmosphere of a French drawing-room is admirably conveyed.

9. Selection H. Hardy's opening of *The Woodlanders* with the traveller on the road to Little Hintock.

10. Selection M. The passage from Meredith's *Egoist*, in which Sir Willoughby Patterne meditates upon Lætitia Dale's devotion.

In each case we aimed to give neither the most difficult nor the easiest passages from the ten novel- **Aims and** ists, but, so far as possible, typical pas- **methods** sages. Obviously, they show decided dif- **in the test** ferences in quality, and in the natural difficulties of approach. But they do not, in any sense, form a reading scale, since we should need thousands of readers to standardize a scale. Our object was not to show grades of difficulty in a series of readings, except incidentally as they might be indicated roughly. Our aim was rather to show how much our students varied their rates in reading, and whether our most understanding readers were reading at a uniformly fast rate, or varied their rates for different authors, and similarly how much our mediocre and poor readers were adapting their speed, or using a fixed rate. We were obliged, therefore, to use simple comprehension checks along with the mimeographed selections. The degree of comprehension achieved was shown by options on a multiple-choice test on a separate sheet, clipped to the appropriate selection. These questions tested, in a plain, broad way, the understanding and appreciation of the accompanying text. There was no attempt to make them difficult, abstruse, peculiar, or tricky. The tests were given early in the course, before much reading had been done. Furthermore, the questions were emphasized as little as possible in giving the time-test. Students were told that nothing was at stake in their answers. Term records in no way depended upon them. We were simply giving a chance for silent reading under certain conditions, and took a simple way of asking them to let us know how well they had read on the spot, with a time-limit. Nor was the time-limit managed with any more emphasis than was absolutely necessary. A numbered card was exhibited and changed every five seconds very quietly before each group. When a student had finished the reading of a particular selection, he simply looked up to see what number was being exhibited, recording it on his answer sheet. That gave us his speed. Then he had ample time to look over the questions on the text and check his choice among the answers.

Of course the atmosphere at such a time is charged with a certain amount of nervous tension. We can allow for it in considering the whole test, **Results of** first of all in the lowering of speed. Our **the test** fastest rates went down to a little over three hundred words a minute. We had two hundred and fifty-nine records to use for our final results, after eliminating papers with incomplete data. We first selected the fifty best readers according to their comprehension of what they read, the fifty poorest in the same way, leaving one hundred and fifty-nine classed as mediocre readers. Then we inspected the time-records to find how these fifty best readers varied their reading rates for the different selections, and also how the mediocre and poor readers varied theirs. The results will best be seen in the six graphs prepared for us by Dr. Ella Woodyard of the Department of Psychology, Teachers College, Columbia University.

SIX GRAPHS SHOWING THE RESULTS OF THE
TESTS AS TAKEN BY 259 STUDENTS AT
TEACHERS COLLEGE

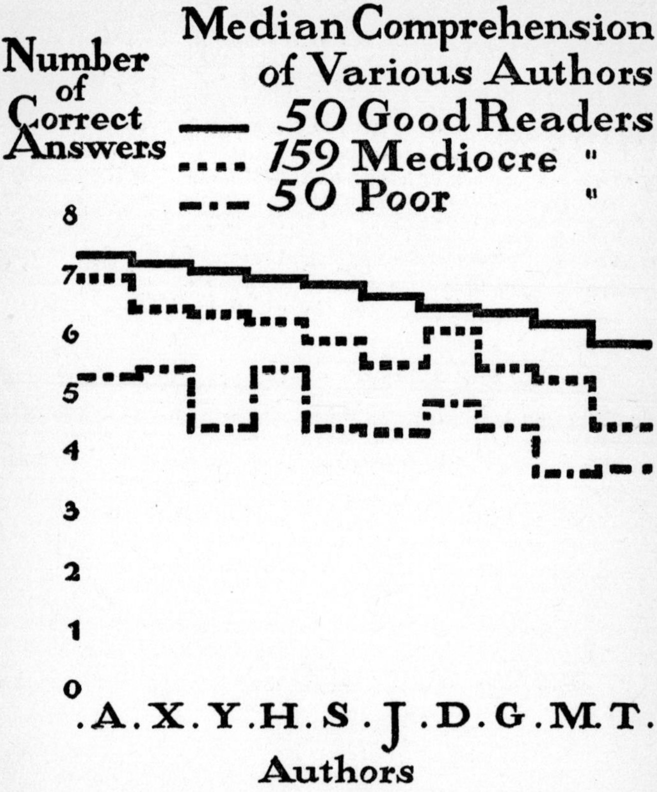

Figure 1. Median Number of
Questions Answered Correctly.

84

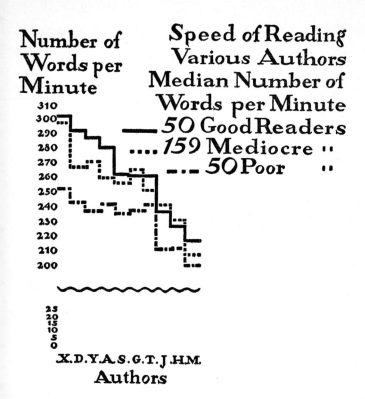

Figure 2. Rates of Reading Various Authors.

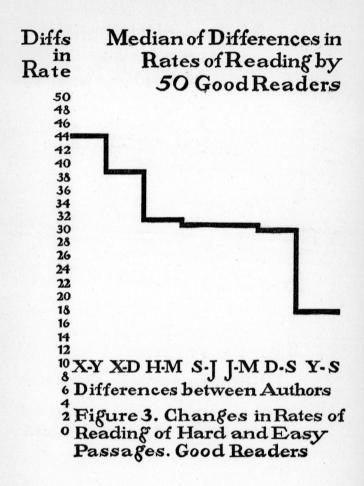

Diffs in Rate

Median of Differences in Rates of Reading by 50 Good Readers

50
48
46
44
42
40
38
36
34
32
30
28
26
24
22
20
18
16
14
12
10
8

X-Y X-D H-M S-J J-M D-S Y-S

6 Differences between Authors

4
2 Figure 3. Changes in Rates of
0 Reading of Hard and Easy
Passages. Good Readers

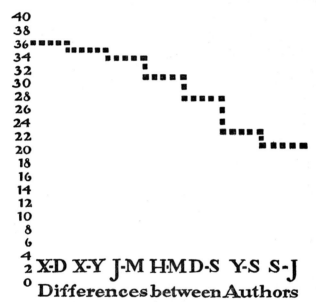

Diffs
in
Rate

Median of Differences in
Rates of Reading by
159 Mediocre Readers

40
38
36
34
32
30
28
26
24
22
20
18
16
14
12
10
8
6
4
2
0

X·D X·Y J·M H·M D·S Y·S S·J

Differences between Authors

Figure 4. Changes in Rates of Reading of Hard and Easy Passages.
Mediocre Readers

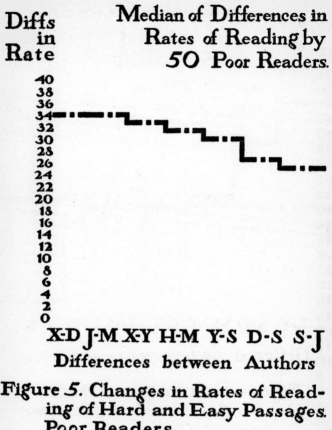

Figure 5. Changes in Rates of Reading of Hard and Easy Passages. Poor Readers

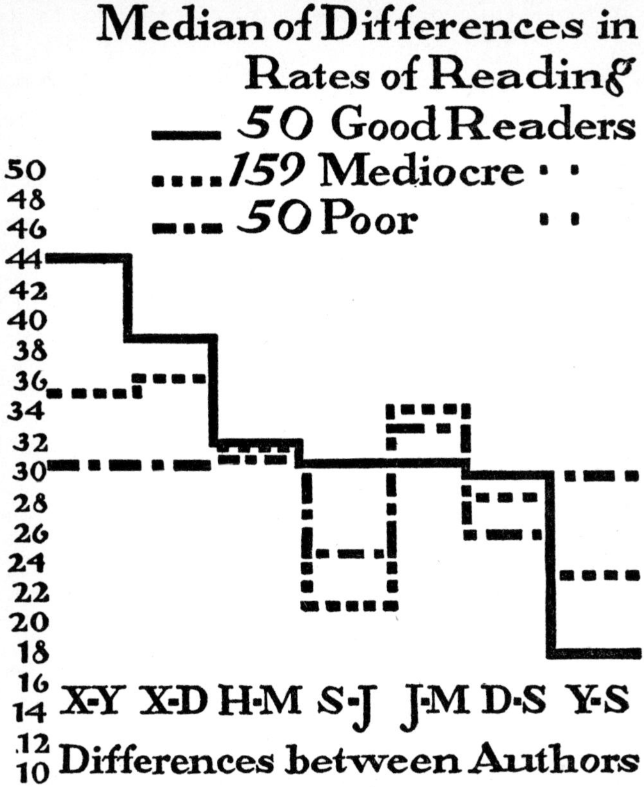

Figure 6. Changes in Rates of Reading of Hard and Easy Passages. Good, Mediocre and Poor Readers

If we glance at Figures 1 and 2, we shall see the comprehension and speed lines of all three classes of readers. The thick, black line of the fifty best readers changes only slightly in the comprehension graph, Figure 1, showing a more constant understanding of what they read, although in Figure 2 their speed line makes a long journey down the page. They are reading Stevenson faster by eighty-five words a minute than they are reading Meredith. Moreover, their line goes down more consistently to the passages in which they tended to find difficulty. Here they are bolder in going slowly at need, so that in the passages from Hardy and James their line is actually below that of the mediocre readers. On the other hand, they take Stevenson fifty words a minute faster than the poor readers do. The line of the mediocre readers follows that of the best readers with less discrimination, while that of fifty poor readers indicated that they go slowly in easy material and then become confused in the difficult passages. Figures 3, 4, and 5 show the medians of differences in rates of reading in all three classes separately, and Figure 6 shows them again together. The pertinent facts can be studied here in detail.

Thus we have here in this simple test the evidence that the most intelligent of our readers have already broken up their fixed reading rates, and have adopted flexible rates, changing according to the difficulty of the material which they are handling. We have also a rough indica- **Helping** tion of the way novels afford sifting-ground **our** **students** for practice in varying rates. Our best **on the** readers who took Stevenson under test con- **basis of** ditions at over three hundred words a min- **the test** ute found that they had something to pause over in Meredith. The way was open for even freer handling of their novel-reading. The rank and file of our readers, the mediocre as we have called them, showed signs of discriminating, but tended to cover the ground with less intelligent variations, some- times feeling hurried and not daring to take a slower rate when needed. They were encouraged at both ends of the line of their novel-reading. They were urged to speed more rapidly when they were simply enjoying narrative, and yet to pause freely when they felt a difficulty, or were impressed by an idea deserving reflection. The slow readers obviously needed very simple narrative to practise on for a time, with encouragement to proceed faster only as they could without hurry or confusion.

The most important single fact that emerged from our test was the thoughtful sincerity in the reading rates of our best readers. Though they could speed over easy ground, they were not bullied by time-cards flashed before them into hurrying over Meredith's difficult allusions, or James's rare art. They refused to make speed in itself a fetish. They could use it or not, as they thought best, even in moments of high tension. The whole question of intelligent handling implies variety in rates. To think carefully over unusual or difficult material is exactly as intelligent as to make fast rates in familiar reading. Indeed it appears rather that speed is a natural result of familiarity, long practice, large reading, and excellent backgrounds of understanding in ordinary matters. The attack on the new, the arresting, the difficult, calls for reflection.

The foundation of principles for more specific questions

Having then laid down a foundation of the principles for novel-reading, we can go on to the more specific questions of actual procedure. When shall we skip? When shall we skim? When shall we slow down? When shall we linger? When shall we reflect? When read aloud? When shall we study the novel? How much shall we allow for personality in novel-reading? And what rewards shall we expect in the end?

CHAPTER IV

WHEN SHALL WE SKIP?

The Technique of Skipping

We have seen that novels more than any other reading demand skill and flexibility in changing techniques according to individual objectives. Skipping is one of the most valuable arts if wisely used for certain ends. Before taking up the question of how and when to skip, let us remind ourselves of the general basis of judgment in skipping. Neglect of minor details in reading often secures thoroughness in handling the general outlines of thought, or in grasping the author's main purposes. We can often assume these minor details from the central plan of what we are reading, just as the musician can infer chords. The central plan, purpose, or idea is never to be lost in over-subordination of details. Therefore we can safely build in many details with swift imagination, running ahead of the slow march of the printed page. Such a basis for judgment in skipping applies with more or less accuracy to all

General basis of judgment in skipping

93

reading, but with especial force to novel-reading, since the details in this long, ambling form are apt to be over-numerous. It becomes an excellent practice ground for sifting values rapidly. We have seen how the dramatist writes with fixed limits of time in mind. How much will his audience endure at one sitting? Deeply as he may wish to inflict more, he knows that he can not. Poetry is also a highly concentrated form. The novelist can give free rein to his imagination, and he repeats very easily. He has no check, except the publisher's refusal to print more. Not only does he repeat, but he often draws a favorite theme out into endless small details. Yet it is highly important to have the same swift unity of æsthetic experience in reading a novel that we have in seeing a play. A novel should be taken at a sitting, if possible. Thus the general basis of judgment in skipping, — namely, the neglect of minor details for a strong, central impression, — applies especially to novel-reading.

Not only does this principle apply especially to novel-reading in general, but it extends to current fiction with particular emphasis. We have seen that excellent critics even to-day recommend skipping practically all of it until something of it has been sifted into permanence. Time will sift for the lazy reader,

Special application to current fiction

so that by the time we are octogenarians we shall know which novels of Henry James, of John Galsworthy, or of H. G. Wells (if any) have become classics. There are important considerations against such an attitude, as we have seen in Chapter II. Nevertheless it is worth remembering that many of the novels tumbling out on the world so fast before Christmas each year will never be heard of again after the summer season, and, in the light of this fact, what seems ruthless skipping may be a fine perspective in our reading. We shall thus do the sifting work of time ourselves. And what is it, after all, that time does? A drastic skipping. Year by year the unimportant work goes by the board, while the valuable scenes of human life in novels stand forth in strong relief. For example, out of Samuel Butler's many books, time has chosen only *Erewhon* and *The Way of All Flesh*. Time is ever busy at this quiet dropping out, sifting out, leaving out. So with regard to current fiction, we shall do well to anticipate the verdict of time, so far as we may, and skip wherever our judgment dictates, secure in the principle of neglect for thoroughness. We shall actually become creative readers, developing the public taste that makes the best survive.

Judicious skipping is not an easy art to acquire. It takes long practice to put skill into the very finger tips as they turn the pages for the eye. The significant passages at the beginning of any book, the crisis near the middle, the important last ten pages have sometimes been seized while a good reader is talking about something else, with his fingers running through the pages, or while he is waiting for someone in a drawing-room or an outer office. No exact rules can be given. In general, however, the eye will pick up a bit of conversation extending down the page, or a chapter heading, or a new division of thought. The kind of book will be evident at once to the book connoisseur. One useful example of how *not* to skip can be given. The sort of lesson assignment now happily out-of-date consisted in numbering the exact pages to be read or studied. The assignments looked something like this: —

> Pages 99–111
> Pages 121–149
> Pages 161–198

How carefully we used to turn, in one movement of the hand, to page 99, and read, with our eyes glued to the pages, to the close of page 111, and then, looking only at page numbers, leap over to page 121, with the indistinct feeling that all between page 111 and page 121 must be a kind of poison not meant for us! Intelligent skipping would never take out whole bunches of text like that, without a glance. Intelligent skipping implies letting the eyes pass through the omitted pages perhaps in leaps of five or six, but always with a certain grasp of their contents from hints here and there. For instance, if we decide to omit the hair-splitting theological disputes of the Covenanters in Scott's *Old Mortality* and *The Heart of Midlothian*, we shall have a richer understanding of the characters if we omit only small sections at a time, letting our eyes glance down the pages as our fingers turn them, and reading a few of the points in dispute. We shall then know how futile and out-of-date it all is, and can proceed with the human qualities involved in the story.

It is well to begin our skipping practice with the needless repetitions so often found in novels. The repetitions may be of such varied kinds **Skip** of material that they are hard to classify. **wherever** But perhaps, for convenience, we may **there is** divide them into events, descriptive de- **needless** tails, and ideas. **repetition**

Who has not found himself reading a scene with the sense that he must have opened the book at a chapter already familiar? The same quarrel is going on, almost in the same words, or the hero is drunk

97

again with his tenth cocktail, or the adventuress turns the same clever trick, or, if it is an old-fashioned **I. Repe-** novel, the heroine faints again. To count **tition of** the swoons and fainting-fits in *Pamela* and **events** *Clarissa Harlowe* would be a task worthy of a dissertation, but, without undertaking it, we soon learn that the same scene will be repeated with the same results after each episode beginning like this: "With a smothered groan, she fell to the floor unconscious." We can skip such crises after a time, while we search for some new factor in the story.

Dickens is a great sinner in repetition. His villains usually approach their ends in a series of preparatory scenes almost exactly alike. Bradley Headstone, for example, in *Our Mutual Friend*, follows Lizzie Hexam with the unwelcome persistence of his dark passions in interviews with the main ideas repeated over and over again. In fact, it is always the same interview. Rogue Riderhood sits in his Limestone Hole plotting darkly and melodramatically, but withal tediously in the same phrases and modes. We can surely slur and skip here with no loss. The chancery-court affairs in *Bleak House* with the details of Jarndyce and Jarndyce are prolonged not only until the costs have eaten up the case, but until we know the scenes almost by heart, whenever they appear. Dickens's scenes at the Old Bailey are often repeated. It would be a mistake, however, to suppose that such repetition is an unusual defect. *Don Quixote* has often been called the greatest novel in the world, and yet the tavern scenes are often duplicated, while its English successor, *Tom Jones*, sometimes gives us the same robust adventure over again. Defoe's *Life and Death of Moll Flanders* abounds in scenes that are practically repetitions. Nor do we have to go to the novels of the past for illustrations. A recent novel with much new material may repeat episodes such as the quarrels between Naomi and Emma Downes, her mother-in-law, before the final crisis in Louis Bromfield's character novel, *A Good Woman*. Unless a reader enjoys going over the details he will probably skip Elmer Gantry's liaisons, at least after the third or fourth.

The temptation to repeat descriptive details is very great. Often the novelist either loves or hates the scene extravagantly, and neither feeling is ever conducive to one statement. A recurring cycle of emotions at the mention of a particular spot sets him off, and we have, in effect, the same scene all over again. The reader who has stood once at the corner of Dyar's or Smith's drug store, and patiently sur-

II. Repetition of descriptive details

veyed Main Street in a series of elaborate photographs will rightly refuse to go over the process more than five times again, or more than once again if he is a practised reader. Thackeray loves to linger over the details of Oxford scenes in *Pendennis*. Dickens, again, repeats descriptive detail often like a sort of refrain. Here we must make a slight distinction, for Dickens deliberately works for rhythmical effects in many of his descriptions. He wishes to put us into a certain recurrent mood whenever certain aspects of the story reappear. So the rain falls drip, drip, drip, on the Ghost's Walk, in *Bleak House*, and the fogs roll their mists over the fitful gas jets early in the afternoon in Dickens's London, and the knitting women count the falling heads at the guillotine in the *Tale of Two Cities*. It is a repeated refrain, making a heightened emotional rhythm. This sort of repetition is easy to infer with a glance of the eye, since the words are deliberately identical, and we get the effect at once. Nevertheless it can be over-used. The metaphor of the Golden Dustman with his dust mounds becomes tedious in *Our Mutual Friend*. We can safely skip the chapters which elaborate the metaphor.

In all these matters we shall do well to remember the "idea-cues" which lead to recognition sometimes more swiftly than word-cues. Half a sentence, and we know that Thackeray is off again on the evils of forced marriages, or that George Eliot is beginning her familiar little sermon, "Dear Reader, are you sure you would have done any better than my hero? Remember how complex the problems of the human heart can be and how important it is to pity and understand," and so on. These cues often extend from one novel of an author to another. We are instantly aware of the sameness, and can use our discretion as to skipping. Of course the inveterate Thackeray reader may not choose to skip. He may feel that there is some new turn even in the old thoughts which Thackeray himself called his "dismal preachments." When Fielding gives us some rollicking bit of satire over again, we may wish to pause for it. That is always open to us. On the whole, however, we all hear too many repetitions, and sifting is excellent practice. It is well to penetrate our novelist's point of view early in our reading, and make ourselves deliberately conscious of it, at least, when it recurs. This habit will serve us well also in appreciating the masterpieces of art in fiction which preserve such economy that we must be aware the first time or not at all.

Closely allied to an actual, verbal repetition may be any passage typical of its kind. Originality is

III. Repetition of ideas

rare and difficult to sustain long. Even the most unusual novel material may be preceded or followed by a situation centuries old. The novelist does not necessarily mean to steal anything. He simply repeats processes long familiar in typical scenes. When the brave but simple Yukon miner closes with the defaulting cashier in the hut already in flames, when the heroine says "One step, and I fire!" or threatens to plunge the dagger into her own breast, or to hurl herself from the parapet, when the cool, fascinating gambler with the tall figure in well-cut evening clothes captivates the high-born lady, when the drunken count sells his family portraits, we are reminded again of the witticism of William Dean Howells to the effect that these scenes have happened so often in fiction and drama that they might some day begin to happen in real life. They form, in other words, a kind of ready reservoir of memories on which any author can draw quite unconsciously when he is fatigued with the concentration of more creative work, or temporarily embarrassed with his difficult characters. He has put them into new situations, and he does not know how to get them out. Presto! A flood, or a suicide, or tuberculosis in the old manner will take off any inconvenient remaining figures. Now the reader also

Skip wherever the story is typical of its kind

102

acquires a reservoir of memories. He soon begins to know these old devices. He will be wise to skip or hurry over them at will.

Very few novelists are entirely free from such unconscious borrowing. Not only sensational fiction, but the psychological novel as well, may give us suddenly a scene whose ending we know at a glance.

A good example of this may be found in the bestseller of several years ago, A. S. M. Hutchinson's *If Winter Comes*. The first half of the novel gives us a tragic conflict of temperaments, with delicate, ironical effects. We watch Mark Sabre, the helpless gentleman whose fine humor is entirely lost on his wife, Mabel, with her conventional patterns of behavior laid out like box hedges. She cannot follow even his mild little joke about the maids, High Jinks and Low Jinks. We see him more and more entangled, unable to grasp the ironies of his life, because he cannot realize crude human nature, nor anything outside the gentleman's code. Now after an admirable exposition of the maladjustment which chiefly concerns Mark Sabre and his wife, and should naturally either be solved or tragically fail *on the inside* (since the situation is preëminently an inward difficulty of impossible rela-

Illustrations of this principle — If Winter Comes

103

tionship between two people), suddenly we have the difficult dilemma broken from the *outside*, by a story with high spots for the servants' hall or a Bowery movie palace. We have Mark Sabre in court for a supposed crime with a girl out of his class. Of course one sees that Mr. Hutchinson wishes to show Mark Sabre the gentleman in every attitude, even in the dock. But this court melodrama is very old. The point under discussion, however, is not the merit of the case, but the reader's approach. Shall we read the latter half of this story with the same attention which we have put upon the first? Not if we discriminate. We can safely skip whole sections here, and find ourselves just exactly where we thought we should be, when we open the page again, well on towards the end of the book. Here are some original notes at the close, and it is always wise to note the close.

Warwick Deeping's *Kitty*, on the other hand, shows an old situation first. Some readers have **Warwick** been misled into dropping the book be-**Deeping's** cause the first chapters dilate upon the *Kitty* familiar war-time marriage of the officer with a shopgirl, the cold fury of the high-born English mother, the discreet plot to separate them, the intercepted letters, etc., etc. Just as Kitty calls on the mother-in-law and is not received we are about to drop the book, when something unusual in the girl spurs us on. She is dealing with this situation broadmindedly. She can see beyond her own pain, with some magnanimity. She tries to understand instead of taking refuge in self-pity. We begin to observe with interest her more original methods, especially since her own mother rescues the situation with practical sympathy. We are surprised to see a portrait of a mother not eaten up with jealousy of her daughter, nor shoving her aside, in the manner so fashionable in Freudian fiction. This mother, shopkeeper that she is, plans and thinks with her children, even her girls. We are intrigued, and we read on. But the real book begins at the eighth or ninth chapter.

Swinnerton's *Nocturne* breaks into two parts even more abruptly. The *Nocturne*, well named from the misty night on the Thames, where the **Swinner-** blurred lights give a kind of magic to the **ton's** dim outlines of tall ships' rigging, applies *Nocturne* properly to the girl Jenny, and her one leap at joy in the few hours with her lover on his ship, with only the fog-horns and distant boat-calls to break the spell. Morning finds Jenny alone again, at work in a drab London suburb, with a memory of one night, — a Nocturne. She may never even hear of her lover again. It is a long, dusty road ahead of her at best. Now to accentuate Jenny's choice we have her sister, narrow, jealous, simple, dreaming only of suburban domesticity. A mere flash of this would be enough for the reader. Instead, we have the tedious details of the commonplace, to emphasize the contrast. The reader is at liberty to read only so much as presents the contrast to him vividly.

A novel of several seasons ago, Norris's *Bread*, develops the quarrels between husband and wife up **Norris's** to a climax of separation. These quarrels **Bread** centre about the economic independence of woman, and cannot be said to repeat themselves exactly, up to the moment when Martin forbids his wife to earn her living outside. Yet they are so typical that we can skip fifty to a hundred pages in the first half of the book and find ourselves just where we thought we should be, if we open at the climax and then read swiftly through to the conclusion.

A good example of a so-called "mystery" story which can be read with much skipping is Mrs. Rine-**Rine-** hart's *The Breaking Point*. Here is an **hart's** interesting psychological problem. How **The** soon will the hero's lost identity come **Breaking** **Point** back to him? Once we see this breaking point where he suddenly remembers the past, we can discard or skip all the rest, unless we wish to read the purely typical, conventional story of "the other fellow", the girl's acceptance of him, and the rest.

This brings us to the frequent "type" or "stock" characters as they are called on the stage, for the very good reason that they are always "in stock." The designing widow, the jealous mother-in-law, the tricky adventurer, the dare-devil thief, or the simple maiden can always be drawn upon by the novelist as well as by the playwright. The practised novel-reader will follow such characters with recognition rather than with curiosity. "O yes," we say to ourselves, "we know him. He will sell his faked Velasquez to the millionaire." It might be amusing to set down a number of such characters on separate slips, and deal the slips to any chance group of readers, asking each reader to describe the character noted on his slip. Would there be any difficulty, if the slips read somewhat as follows?

> The French count
> The English bobby
> "Cook's man"
> The Italian street singer
> The American millionaire
> The English woman in the Piazza di Spagna
> The floorwalker
> The colored waiter
> The American tourist

"Type" or "stock" characters

Typical characters become the conventional puppets of a novel. It is easy to predict how they will react to circumstances. Especially when the main emphasis is upon the exciting events of a tale, the persons of the story take these well-known shapes. Obviously an exciting crisis cannot be held up by the development of strongly marked individuals. The characters thus become "fillers in" for a framework of breathless action, hair-raising escapes, and so forth. The reader can easily learn to assume and therefore skip or discard a good deal about stock characters, here and there. It will greatly increase speed without destroying pleasure or meaning.

We must be on our guard, however, since these conventional "fillers in" may be accompanied by one or two original characters of vivid reality and power. We must distinguish sharply between the lay figures of James Fenimore Cooper, — his dapper Heywards, Dunwoodies, and Whartons, with their weak females, — and his great triumvirate of the trackless woods, Leatherstocking, Chingachgook, and Uncas. We must read as much about the typical young heroes and heroines as will give us their connections with the great central figures. We need not do more than taste the conventional love affairs, nor

Illustrations of "stock" characters

follow all of Mabel Dunham's silly, helpless behavior in the *Pathfinder*. She is supposedly in good health, but she plays the nervous, startled invalid in the forest, because Cooper's lovely female must, above all, appeal to chivalry. Both Cooper and Scott, according to their time, feared to put any courage or fire into a woman unless she were unclassed like Judith Hutter, or a peasant like Jeanie Deans. Most of Cooper's women, and many of Scott's, are therefore mere puppets to be disregarded for the main current of the novel.

Mysterious villains often come under the same head. Provis in *Great Expectations* is an example. After his dramatic scene with Pip on the Kentish marshes, we are sure that he has a past of crime mingled with noble impulses, and the events which connect him with Pip are easy to infer. His trial is like other favorite scenes at the Old Bailey in Dickens's long repertoire. There will be no loss in slighting it in favor of the superb scenes between Pip and Joe Gargery. We could have no better illustration of the difference between the pathos of Dickens's heightened, theatrical passages, and the haunting, life-like quality of Joe's devotion. It will also save the time of the reader if he learns to watch all mysterious resemblances between characters in fiction.

The chances are ten to one that these persons are the same, or that one will be disguised as the other, or will prove to be the long-lost child of the other. Long before Esther Summerson speaks with her mother's voice in *Bleak House*, we should be sure that she is Lady Dedlock's lost child. It is a typical, conventional device which we should recognize at once, and thus be in possession of the coming events more quickly.

The most quaintly amusing thing about many novelists is their habit of talking like experts in biology, chemistry, agriculture, theology, archæology, geology, mathematics, eugenics, sociology, finance, industry, the League of Nations, and other subjects. The novelist seems peculiar among artists in this trait. Even the Sunday Supplements would hardly invite the sculptor, the portrait painter, or the architect to overflow on heredity. Yet the novelist meets a unique temptation. Unless he is wary, he begins to speak at dinners for all sorts of objects. Clubs and societies lionize him, and listen to his words on any topic. At length he confuses what he does know with what he does not. We have all attended dinners at which some eminent biologist has sat silent while a fluent medley on

With notable exceptions, it is wise to skip scientific, theological, and ethical treatises in the novel

heredity comes across the table from the popular novelist. His mistake is in supposing that his very vivid knowledge of some aspect of human experience extends farther than it does. We all contribute to his mistake, and are partially to blame for it when we listen to him, like disciples.

If it were a mere matter of a little vanity, no essential harm would be done. But what happens to his next novel? These ideas which he has been speaking about are much easier to write in an easy stream than a great human story. That requires intense concentration, a complex construction of scenes, with human characters played off against one another. If he takes less trouble with his story, and merely evolves the ideas of some central figure, how easy and fascinating! He has a form so flexible that it will allow him any sort of autobiographical riot. Let anyone who questions the truth of this process re-read H. G. Wells's *Tono-Bungay*, and see what Wells was doing in 1908. The action will seem so rapid and unencumbered, the characters will seem so varied and so dramatic that one will scarcely recognize the author of *The World of William Clissold*. How aptly the latter is named! Not William Clissold, not even his liaisons, but an account of his world in toto. Business, war, peace, art, wages, socialism, sex. It is interesting autobiography. But the novelist's art has been extinguished.

The novel as an art form emerged historically from long, rambling romances and disjointed, episodic, picaresque adventures. It gathered up essays, sermons, disquisitions of all sorts as it rolled along into a bulky mass. Only now and then in its long history have the inchoate elements been fused by some artist into definite, sculptured effects. If we glance for a moment at other art forms like the sonnet, with its severe restrictions, or the cathedral, with its carefully planned lines, we shall see at once what a chance for individual vagary the novel affords to any dreamer. In fact even great novels are sometimes crowded with digressions. Thus the late nineteenth century had a ready vehicle in literature for all the new interests in science, pseudoscience, and metaphysics. Every theory of the past fifty years has been exploited in some novel.

Tolstoi gives fifty-one pages of *The Kreutzer* **Digres-** *Sonata* to explaining that all sex relations **sions and** are in themselves swinish, and only to **interludes** be reluctantly allowed for producing chil- **in well-** **known** dren. His sex hygiene, the reaction from **novels** his early years, depends solely on a few instances from the corrupt life of the Czarist barracks in Russia. No biologist or psychologist of to-day would be likely to refer to Tolstoi's pages. Yet here are fifty-one in his shortest, most concentrated novel. The long discourses to the same effect in *Resurrection*, even the digressions in *Anna Karenina*, add many more. Gogol's *Dead Souls* has long discussions of outmoded governmental and political technique, along with more picturesque lyrical interludes such as the impassioned address to "Russia, my country", comparing her to the bold, dashing troïka, plunging headlong to — what? Samuel Butler spends seventy-five pages before the crisis in *The Way of All Flesh* to explain the conflict between High and Low Church parties in the established English church after the Oxford movement. Olive Schreiner halts the action in her novel, *From Man to Man*, while for an entire chapter of fifty-two pages, called *Raindrops in the Avenue*, her heroine, on an African farm where she has practically no knowledge of the outside world, meditates on Greek ideas of the fourth century before Christ, on Greek, Assyrian, Egyptian, and Indian art, on class distinctions in the ancient world, on social growth, racial prejudices, the opium trade, distinctions between Asiatic and European races, the Chinese ideal of old age, physiology, and love. George Moore revels in æsthetic appreciation of medieval music in *Evelyn Innes*, and we hear a great deal of the revival of Palestrina, Vittoria, and the "Missa Brevis", the reading of quaint motets and the playing of Elizabethan virginals. The Mass of Pope Marcellus takes an important place in the story, as also do the vocal masses of the sixteenth century. Romain Rolland discusses the operas of Wagner at length in *Jean Christophe*. These are all novels of distinction,

There is, therefore, no strict limitation of subject even in justly famous novels. When we come to the so-called historical novel, we have chapter after chapter which might be in a historical textbook, but not, as a rule, in a good text! The subject matter often needs definite counteracting, in fact, lest the pictures of Louis XI, Queen Elizabeth, Marie Antoinette, and others should become fixed ideas in young minds. We shall treat the reading of historical novels as a whole in another chapter. The point at issue for the moment is the definite insertion of historical material in a novel. Obviously, it should not be taken too seriously in any case, even when it has a good deal of environmental æsthetic value. Sometimes the artist himself does not take it too seriously. Victor Hugo's famous chapters on the topography and architecture of old Paris have penetrated even the composition textbooks. Yet he himself did not trouble to re-write a long section on

Notre Dame for the first edition when the pages had
been lost.   After they had been found, he inserted
them into the next edition, in the hope that they
might prove interesting to the readers who care for
artistic and historical settings, although he admitted
that they were not necessary to the story.   A good
deal of historical material about the days of Louis
Philippe creeps into *Les Misérables*, along with the
twenty-three pages describing the network of old
sewers in Paris.   Genealogical details as well as
historical summaries are mingled in Thackeray's
Henry Esmond.   Probably any teacher of English
literature could be safely challenged to give the
Esmond genealogy in detail without looking again
at the book.   If that be true for the teacher, what
are we to say to the young reader for whom the
book will surely begin with the forlorn little fellow,
Master Henry Esmond, wandering in the great hall
and waiting to be presented to the Viscountess of
Castlewood on page 27?   As to Sir Walter Scott's
romances, they usually begin at about the third
chapter, after prefaces, long introductions, explana-
tory epistles, and two chapters of historical material.
Typically, it is in the third chapter that the familiar
solitary horseman reins up in the courtyard of some
old tavern, or before the drawbridge of some gloomy
castle at dusk.   Exceptions such as *The Talisman*,

where we find our horseman at once on the desert sands, or *Kenilworth*, where he alights at the bonny Black Bear in Cumnor on the second page, only fix the general custom in Scott's novels more firmly in mind.

Hitherto we have been discussing insertions and digressions having some bearing on the events or the characters of the tale. The historical chapters give a background for the action; scientific chapters show us the problems which fill the hero's mind; critical chapters on music, architecture, painting, sculpture, and the drama provide a kind of environmental action of æsthetic influences on the hero. But there are episodes and interludes with little or no discoverable earthly connection with any part of the novel. Such stories within stories have a fascination for the author who lets them draw him off his main track. Fiction of the first order may have both episodes and discussions quite remote from the theme. It would puzzle any reader to explain how Cardenio's recovery of Lucinda in *Don Quixote* bears on the fortunes of the Knight of La Mancha. Dostoiefsky prefaces the touching salute of Father Zossima to the wayward Dmitri in *The Brothers Karamazoff* with a long account of the principles, organization, procedures, and beliefs of his monastery, and of Greek Christianity in general.

These facts have no influence on the story whatever, since even Alyosha has responded only to the central ideals of Christianity, and the other characters not even to these. Dostoiefsky took an interest in the history and relations of the monastery, and simply let himself write as he pleased. The same temptation occasionally visits writers known especially for their restrained artistic coherence. Tom Outland's story of his adventure on the mesa in *The Professor's House* of Miss Willa Cather is a little polished gem in itself. But inserted into the professor's subtle emotional distress, it has no meaning except possibly as a contrasting movement, which intensifies that distress. In any case it breaks the reader's warming interest unwarrantably, when a few words would have sufficed for its essential meaning. Mrs. Wharton also comes close to the same kind of digression when she repeats the incidents of the fakirs, in *Twilight Sleep*. George Meredith takes fifteen pages in *The Amazing Marriage* to review the story of the postilion, Charles Dump, as to whether it was Curtis Fakenham who pursued the Countess of Cressett and Captain Kirby when they eloped. We even have a description of Charles Dump's portrait. And neither the postilion nor the portrait ever enters again. Meredith interrupts his novels constantly with obscure allusions, speculations, and

meanderings of Dame Gossip or the Black God-
dess Fortune, quotations from imaginary books of
maxims, ancient authorities, and curious riddles or
epigrams. These often have very slight, if any,
connection with the characters of the story, and
help to explain why our students always find Meredith the most difficult of all novelists.

If now we ask any group of readers what they do
about insertions, digressions, and scientific treatises
in novels, we shall find an amusing variety
of response. There will be the reader who
skips all of them. There will be the reader
who takes every word of anything which
he reads at all. There will be all varieties between
these extremes. "I always read every word of
Romain Rolland's criticism of music," says the
student of music. "I read every word about Arrow-
smith's work in germs, because I can't help reading
anything of that sort which my eye lights upon,"
says the student of medicine. "It would be a crime
to miss Victor Hugo's description of the rose window
in Notre Dame," says the artist. "No matter how
inaccurate the historical facts may be, I always
study the setting of Scott's novels," says the student
of history. "Visit old scenes in Paris, and not read
Victor Hugo's account of the old city?" asks the
conscientious traveller. "But Samuel Butler's ac-

Criteria for skipping digressions

118

count of High and Low Church conflict bears on actual English problems today! We should read it," says the student of current affairs. Such replies will take us back at once to one of the general criteria for reading novels, discussed in Chapter II. We read novels not only with the author's purpose but with our own purposes. When any subject matter hits a special interest we shall have every right to appropriate it for our own purposes. I may well choose to read Hawthorne's description of the famous room in the Capitoline where the Marble Faun after Praxiteles is kept, if I am on my way to Rome for the first time. If I am going to Edinburgh, I may choose to read every detail which Scott gives us about the old Tolbooth or Heart of Midlothian. If I am a specialist in the Stuart Wars, I may choose to read all the Esmond family history.

For the general reader who has no such special interest, it will be wise to return to another common basis for judgment, — namely, the author's purpose. Obviously, there is great variety in the mass of material in interludes and digressions. Some of it has no discoverable connection with the theme of the novel, or with the author's main purpose. On the other hand, much of it may have direct or indirect bearing on the lives of his characters. It explains their æsthetic, or moral, or intellectual, or social environment; and this environmental æsthetic value may be highly important in the author's purpose. He wants us to feel the whole beauty, or the whole tragedy, or the whole comedy of the situation which must be interpreted by the play and interplay of many ideas and social forces. For example, Galsworthy's *Forsyte Saga* explains Soames Forsyte to us by showing us the many complex influences of family ideas, social approvals or disapprovals, economic conditions, even æsthetic fashions in picture galleries. Through the course of his whole life, from the time of his young manhood in *The Man of Property*, to his *Swan Song*, we watch these influences acting upon a malleable family type. At no time could we point to any discussion and say, "This has nothing to do with the author's purpose." It does all serve to explain or to react upon the Forsyte family. Therefore, if we apply this criterion of the author's purpose, we shall not skip much of *The Forsyte Saga*, unless we decide that for us Galsworthy accomplished his purpose a trifle sooner than he thought he did. Suppose that the author's purpose is to show the tragic breakdown of life in a sordid, degraded atmosphere like that of the Karamazoff family. It will be important to explain the outside influences on the children, of course.

Even though one son, Alyosha, escapes the corruption because of his pure stream of Christian feeling, that does not necessitate writing the history of a monastery. Such a discussion jumps the track of the author's purpose entirely. We have a right to see a difference in principle here, and, almost for the sake of getting Dostoiefsky's magnificent purpose in a clear unity, to skip his digression.

One more help in deciding when to skip digressions may be found in the simple question, "Does the author know anything about the subject?" Obviously there is a great deal of difference between wading through a discussion by an amateur, and the treatment of an expert, or at least a serious student of the subject. For example, Romain Rolland is a distinguished musical critic, author of books and articles on Beethoven, Handel, and the opera in general. Victor Hugo knew his old Paris and its Gothic architecture far beyond any amateur stage. If we pause for his chapters on topography and gargoyles, we shall be justified by generations of appreciation. If we choose to go straight through his novels first for the thrill of the tale and the unified impression, we may be even more justified to go back to the chapters on old Paris and read them as a separate unit. They are worth it. We can note in passing, here, that these illustrations are taken from the work of artists who are writing of some art kindred to their own, and of which they have some critical knowledge as well as appreciation, helpful to the reader. In the matter of scientific discussions, even where the material seems fairly sound, the general reader may be pardoned for preferring the excellent scientific monographs written by experts and now available to the public.

The author's main plan, theme, purpose will guide us very helpfully in skipping descriptions. If we put the central idea of the novel in a single sentence for ourselves just as soon as it emerges from the pages to us (and the practised reader will seize the central theme of any book very early in the reading), we shall have an excellent, although not infallible, test for the introduction of unnecessary descriptive detail. We shall be reassured by the fact that well-known artists have used the same measuring rod themselves before sending out their material. In a sense, the creative reader follows the same processes as the creative writer. Turgenev cut down stories three and four times in the writing, until every superfluous word was gone, and every word that remained carried all the weight of meaning and suggestion possible. The main theme

Criteria for skipping descriptions

is thus sifted out of nature into art. After all, we only help our novelist who has not pruned away his luxuriant overgrowths, when we do a little of it for him.

Descriptions are especially dangerous temptations for the novelist, since he often has an autobiographical interest in them. And whoever wished to be brief in his life-history? A conscientious artist like Arnold Bennett tells us in his preface to *The Old Wives' Tale* that he himself had lived as a child in the seventies in the actual draper's shop of the Baines family. No wonder that he knew every passage, every closet, the show-room over the millinery and silken half of the shop, and the exact situation of every kind of cloth. We could almost draw up a deed of sale for that shop. In *Clayhanger* he gives nine pages to the new machines in the printing office. Thackeray's slow chronicle of Pendennis's life in Oxford has many autobiographical details. They are connected with the main theme chiefly by the author's own personal interest in them. Compare such scenes with the picture of Major Pendennis at breakfast at his club in Pall Mall. Like an etching in five or six strokes the Major sits there in his buff waistcoat with the King's crown on the buttons, his well-fitting coat, his white gloves, his whiskers, his cane, his long white wristbands, and his ring emblazoned with the arms of Pendennis. He needs only to survey his letters through his gold double eyeglass as he waits for his toast and he is complete. Or take another example of good description in *Clayhanger*, after Arnold Bennett has the story in the grip of Edwin's grim experience at his father's death-bed. The reader shares every despairing breath in the fight between life and death. Yet very little happens in the sick-room. It is almost pure description. Such instances show how much difference in the quality and handling of material can be found within even famous novels, so that it becomes impossible to adapt any one technique of reading to all parts of a novel alike, except in rare cases. When we judge that an author is running into details of his own history which have a slender connection with the main theme, we shall be justified in skipping, according to our principle. On the other hand, we should not miss a word of the significant detail in the Major's portrait, since it places him for us at once in the scheme of things.

One of our students made the naïve suggestion that we should read descriptions only if the author is an artist at that sort of thing. We cannot make such a sweeping rule as that, since, as we have just seen, a fine artist may be uneven in his work. Yet, broadly speaking, we may demand artistic quality in descriptive material. This does not mean that the scene must be pretty. It may have elements of horror, but we demand an artistic quality in the way these elements are blended into significance, into an impressive total. We must feel, see, hear, smell, and taste vividly, and the scene withal must have its influence on human life in the story. We shall not follow merely pointless walks down Piccadilly or St. James's street just to get our hero somewhere. We shall ask to feel our London as Hugh Walpole makes us feel it in *Wintersmoon*, as Thackeray can always make us feel it. Mere recital of geographical names will not do. Mere names abound, for instance, in the Countess Bibesco's *Catherine Paris*. We can slur and skip them, especially since most of them belong to the day of pre-war Europe. But though the hunting scenes in Turgenev's *Sportsman's Sketches* belong not only to a pre-war Europe, but to a Russia that is forever gone, we shall make a mistake to lose the exquisite touches by which the freshness of the forest is set over against the human misery of the peasants. We shall miss something of the exotic flavor of Java and the East if we do not read the description of Java Head in Hergesheimer's novel of that name. It is not necessary to look up all the fruits mentioned,

125

if we do not know them. We shall get the exotic flavor all the better for the picturesque strangeness. We shall taste the mystery and romance of the East, as well as the beauty of old Salem in the days of its clipper ships. Such passages as Galsworthy's account of the Forsyte parlor — a family mausoleum down to the departed Aunt Anne's last stool and tidy — will need even closer reading, without the loss of a word. More profound novels wherein Nature becomes part of the environing action, a protagonist as important as any social influence, will more appropriately be considered in a later chapter.

Skipping is a valuable art, as we have tried to show. It not only saves the reader's time in these days when valuable reading matter comes faster than we can handle it, but the practice will make us keener in discriminating the poor from the commonplace, and the commonplace from the good. If we make a few mistakes, they are less costly in the reading of novels in general, than in the reading of other literature. Above all, we return to the personal reference. It is a highly individual matter to grade our reading rates and our skipping according to particular needs. It is often just a personal choice. Yet even if we differ as to the passages to be skipped, there will surely be some guidance for the intelligent reader in the general principles of skipping clear repetitions, typical scenes, obvious interludes, discussions unrelated to the main purpose or unnecessary to it, and commonplace, tedious details.

CHAPTER V

WHEN SHALL WE TASTE AND SKIM?

Never has variety in our reading techniques been so important as it is to-day, in a world of increasing complexity, with more demands upon the reader's attention than he can meet without ready skills. He must give up once and for all the idea of reading everything straight ahead. There are varied approaches which will be useful. Even skipping the pages under our hands should imply a glance at the titles of chapters, sub-headings, page headings, and a leading sentence now and then. A further step consists in what we may call tasting a book. This means a rapid survey of its contents, with attention to all the chapter headings, and to the opening paragraphs of all chapters, with a fast reading of the first chapter or section, possibly a little slower reading of the central chapters, which make the heart of the book, and a rapid concluding glance at the end. The reviewer who speaks of "tearing the heart out of a book" often refers to this kind of

Skipping, skimming, and testing. Differences illustrated

tasting. Readers who have never tried it, and who would naturally regard it as superficial, are hereby urged to make one attempt, and watch the results. They will probably be surprised at the clearness of their impressions of the book. Tasting for some purposes may be as valuable as slow reading is for other purposes.

Another valuable skill in reading may be called skimming the pages. Skimming means reading at one's top speed, without pausing to take the individual words, phrases, or sentences consciously, but leaping by paragraph units, or, with practice, even by page units. The eye moves so rapidly that the whole page is flashed before it in what seems like one sweep but in reality probably means two or three slight, almost imperceptible pauses at the paragraph breaks. A fast skimmer has his right forefinger always at the top of the page and seems to turn each page almost as fast as he comes to it.   In reality, several seconds elapse, unless he is skipping.

Current fiction affords especially good chances to use all these habits profitably. For instance, one picks up the Countess Bibesco's novel, *Catherine Paris*. The first few chapters put an admirably fresh theme before us, the romantic longing for a place that suggests the beauty of life, as Paris suggests it to Catherine. Paris is her love and the

French lover is only her symbol of Paris and France. We taste this in the first third of the book. Then we find many chapters developing Catherine's wanderings over Europe, exiled by her Austrian passport from the country of her soul. We infer the meaning of them. We look through these long chapters, forming the central portion of the book, and reaching well into the last third. We read only a page here and there. We pick up the scene of her impassioned meeting with her French lover. We leave her planning French citizenship at last for her son. We have only tasted the book, since we have read the opening chapters, seized the theme, the crisis, and the conclusion. Yet we feel confident that our tasting has given us the essential values in the novel, because we grasped the problem well enough to infer the long elaboration of it. Skimming, on the other hand, means going straight ahead, as one would be inclined to do in reading Hugh Walpole's *Wintersmoon*, so limpid, so easy, so charming that it can be covered in an hour and a half, with the omission of only a night or two of the heroine's anguish. From these instances it will be clear that skipping, tasting, and skimming make an excellent combination of techniques to apply to the current novels which are important to examine for many reasons, but may not be important enough to read in their entirety.

We should at least taste twenty or thirty novels of the season's output every year.

In general, when we are using light fiction for pure relaxation, we can let out our top speed with no conscience. Since our purpose is to be amused, and the author's purpose is to amuse us, why accept boredom or pains? Incidentally we shall be developing a higher rate **Skim light fiction in general** of speed, and learning to use this maximum rate freely, while we are getting amusement and relaxation. If this somewhat Pecksniffian attitude does not suggest too much self-conscious complacency, we may add to it the pleasure of looking for familiar types of character in light fiction. Our students have enjoyed the fun of reporting such well-known figures as they begin to observe them after a little training. Ready recognition of them saves time in more serious reading, for we can slur them wherever they appear, or at least take them very easily, swiftly, and lightly. Some of them enter the finer novels, as we have seen, and when we are prepared for them by our lighter reading, we shall gain in economy of time and effort for our serious reading. Light fiction which usually centres about action, danger, escapes, and thrills, abounds in stock characters which are in reality puppet figures for the play of exciting events. There they are, — the adventurer, the illiterate millionaire, the heroine who finds her career dust and ashes, etc., etc. Even though, in the *Saturday Evening Post*, their habitat is more likely to be Hollywood than the Balkans, they themselves have not changed much. It will rather add to the reader's fun to list them mentally as he reads.

Detective fiction has taken a sudden stride into more artistic form in the past few years. It is extremely helpful for the slow reader. We have found that students who need more speed will be helped by this form more than by the pure adventure story. A good detective novel will not let us halt at the individual sentences or even paragraphs. We are on the scent, and we take the trail with the sleuth hounds. We hardly care to pause for the characterizations. Perhaps this is fortunate, since most of the characters are conventional lay figures for the mystery. For instance, while the heroines of fiction in general have been altering with many phases of the woman movement, the heroine of the detective thriller remains blissfully unaware of change. She faints, trembles, shrieks, and has to be lifted to the couch just as if she had stepped out of Cooper or Scott. An exception in a modern girl like Sibylla in S. S. Van Dine's *The Greene Murder Case* makes one fearful that she may be the murderess. Strength of purpose is familiar enough in the vampire of detective and mystery fiction. The probability of her power is never questioned even when she can outwit all the leading officials of Scotland Yard. In Marie Belloc Lowndes's novel, *The Story of Ivy*, Ivy looks up at the commissioner of police and his mind ceases to function. Ivy is typical, not individual. Every character in Agatha Christie's *Mystery of the Blue Train* is typical in the same sense. Not one is individualized. Yet these novels are among the best of their class. Therefore the reader will rush on through his detective mystery without needing to watch for any fresh character interest, or to pause for any subtle play of relationship. He will get most out of it by reading it just as fast as he can enjoy it.

Not only light fiction, but also romantic fiction, even of a high order, should be skimmed. How can we hope to seize the quality of *The Three Musketeers*, of *Treasure Island*, of *Kidnapped*, of *The Count of Monte Cristo*, of *The Queen's Necklace*, of *The Man in the Iron Mask*, if we pause where *they* never **Romances need high speed if not actual skimming** pause, if we analyze where *they* never analyze? We must read at the pace of these galloping heroes, if we are really to share their experiences, and live their breathless moments with them. When we are with Dantès thrown in a sack from the Château d'If down to the boiling waves below, when D'Artagnan has

133

left his wounded behind on the road from Paris to Calais, and crosses the channel in disguise for the diamonds of the Queen, when the same invincible hero is taking General Monk in a deal box to meet the King, when Jeanne de Valois and the Cardinal de Rohan so nearly entrap Marie Antoinette, we shall be using a kind of perpetual slow-movement film if we linger and hold up the suspense. That is to say, we shall have no sense of rapid action at all, but only a kind of statuesque pose in mid-air. Just here the schools have made their worst blunder in teaching literature. There are still texts which provide for shutting off the omnivorous readers who have "gone ahead in the story", keeping the discussion down to the minutest points of one chapter in the midst of some breathless situation, and treating a hasty council of doughty rogues as if it were the agenda of the League of Nations. We have spoiled the love of literature by such methods. Our college students often have an aversion to all classics read in high school. That is why it has seemed best to make a fresh attack, and urge deliberately rapid reading of all romances. When readers once feel free to seize the horror of that broken tower-stair for David Balfour without reading the history of Scotland, to enjoy *The Vicomte de Bragelonne* without analyzing the royal finances, they begin to widen the horizons of their reading vigorously. They have acquired a new technique for romantic fiction, which they proceed to apply to whatever of this sort comes in their way, whether it be *The Prisoner of Zenda*, *Rupert of Hentzau*, or a novel of Weyman or Ibañez, treated in broad, splashing colors never meant to be taken minutely or slowly. The reading of romantic novels should follow a diagram something like this:

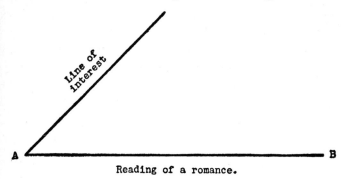

Reading of a romance.

The so-called historical novel usually merges into the romantic type, with some exceptions like the scholarly *Romola* of George Eliot. Ordinarily we should apply the same rapid-reading skill which we use for a romance. We may have more scruples about doing so because there seems to be much sober history involved. We have an uneasy feeling about skipping or neglecting it. Of course it is open to the

Historical novels also need very rapid reading

intelligent reader to choose along the lines of his own interests. If he chooses to ignore a considerable amount of the purely historical material, he will not be superficial necessarily in his attitude towards history. Indeed, his respect for historical accuracy might lead him to place less emphasis on the treatment of history in a novel. The historical novel is a hybrid form, neither history nor novel, but far more novel than history. All sorts of liberties with fact are taken easily by the author. For example, Amy Robsart had been dead several years when Queen Elizabeth held the revels at Kenilworth. After all, what difference does it make to our enjoyment of the romantic color, the stir of life and pageantry, the vivid personal portraits? A sense of the movement and quality of life in a past time is a valuable aid to historical imagination. To scrutinize too closely may be misleading us on the very track of history itself.

Once our students have seen what *Quentin Durward* means when it is taken in three or four hours instead of three or four weeks, they begin to recover Sir Walter Scott as he certainly meant himself to be taken. The master of the "big bow-wow" style would be disconcerted if he could see the volumes of notes for studying the texts which he wrote off in white heat so rapidly and so bravely to pay his debts.

When we can survey the marvellous portrait of Louis XI, a worthy match in literature for the painting of Innocent X by Velásquez in the Doria at Rome, and regard the work as one of imagination enlivened by the picturesque settings of the fifteenth century, we shall have perhaps a valuable stimulus to the study of history, but we shall be enjoying a novel for its own sake, frankly as literature.

This sort of æsthetic enjoyment becomes easier and more natural in reading historical novels written with more care than Scott used. Dumas, on the whole, wrote with more attention to the art of his story, though his novels have many incongruities. Gogol's *Taras Bulba* is a fine example of what the type could become, if it were confined simply to a romantic flavor of the past, enlivened by heroic figures like the gigantic old Taras Bulba the Cossack, dying in torture and yet hurling defiance at his foes. So rapid and tremendous is the tramp of movement in this novel, that it would be hard to devise a technique to slow down the reading. Yet one does undoubtedly recover something of the atmosphere of medieval Little Russia. Sigrid Undset, the Norwegian novelist writing powerfully of medieval Norway in the thirteenth century, is also discarding the direct use of history, as she develops her story with rapid movement. The picturesque scenes of Norwegian life emerge with vividness, but only incidentally as a part of the developing action. *The Axe* has a memorable Christmas mass throwing its tapers on to the deep snow-drifts and black branches without the Church, yet we read it very rapidly. It is merely a swift incident in the life of the hero. There is no discussion of medieval customs. They simply appear in their natural setting. Probably this form of historical imagination will become more popular as time goes on.

So far the selection of novels for skimming or very rapid reading has been easy. Before one reaches the end of the second chapter, one knows whether any book is romantic in general treatment or not. It will not take much effort to go swiftly after that, since it is natural to follow the excitement of adventure with rapid rates of reading. One needs only to abandon scruples, and to release one's natural speed. There is, however, a kind of novel more difficult to define, much more subtle in treatment and effect, yet just as definitely requiring a swift unity of impression to be appreciated. It is the novel depicting the course of a single consuming passion or mood, with such intensity that it gathers a momentum like that of action. Very little may happen, in this novel, and what does happen is sub-

Read novels of simple, impassioned mood swiftly

ordinate, absorbed in the white heat of some longing, or fear, or hate, or love. The reader is caught
up into the experience, until he does not seem to
be reading so much as living with the characters.
Their experience throbs in him. He scarcely knows
whether he is reading fast or slowly. Yet when he
looks at the clock he will find that the novel has not
taken more than an hour and a half, or two hours at
the most. For some readers it may be only an hour.

François Mauriac's *Thérèse* is such a novel. Thérèse is a girl of the farming gentry in the "landes",
the salt marshes near Bordeaux, where wealth consists of tall pines and scrub timber. We see the
tossing branches in the dark December rains as
Thérèse saw them, we feel the heat of the white
sandy roads in summer as Thérèse felt them. We
are scarcely conscious of reading descriptions at all.
We simply feel these things, along with Thérèse's
tormented longing for escape. Not to be a house-
wife counting her acres, giving family dinners, receiving the abbé, but to have some world of beauty,
knowledge, understanding, depth, passion! We follow her revolt, her despair, her punishment, her
strange release, not as events but as aspects of the
dark torture of Thérèse's whole being.

Another novel of this sort is Julian Green's *Closed
Garden*, in which a young French girl is losing her

balance in a lonely house and garden. How we feel the sunny silence of that garden! If the bee hums, if the gate clicks, it seems loud. How terrible the ticking of that clock when she has luncheon alone in the dining room! There is no escape until at last she is found in a country road, unable to give her name. The analysis throughout is rapid, and needs rapid reading for the effect of intense mental suffering, growing rapidly worse up to the end.

The Mother, by Grazia Deledda, is a good example of the same rise of feeling to a high pitch. Very little actually happens in this novel with its scene in a little Sardinian village perched on a crag above the deep valley. The young priest is caught up by the temptation of passionate love and we feel his desperate struggles within. Outside is the contrasting quiet of the clear, sunny Sardinian day. It is so still that the ringing of the woodchopper's axe can be heard from the mountain side. The young priest attends the sick and the dying as usual. His acolyte knows no difference. Yet the ceaseless struggle within leaves the reader breathless. When the sharp conflict has cleared, it is not the priest who has suffered most after all. His old peasant mother is dead in her place at mass, from sympathy and suspense. The tragedy, as swift as a Southern storm, needs to be read for a single impression. Turgenev's *Smoke* has a similar quality.

Wild Geese, by Martha Ostenso, carries us forward in a rapid crescendo of the hate and defiance felt by all the members of a family for the brutal peasant father. The culminating peak of the story has more action in this case. But it is the movement of intense, human feeling which makes the reading rapid. In all these instances we have one dominating passion of fear, or longing, or hate. Therefore the theme has a certain simplicity. There are no subtle connections to make us pause and reflect in the process of the reading.

Thus we see that in approaching light fiction, the story of adventure, the detective thriller, the romance, the historical novel, and the novel with one dominant emotional strain, we may profitably use our fastest reading rates.

CHAPTER VI

WHEN SHALL WE LINGER AND REFLECT?

If one has climbed to that lofty room where the enthroned Virgin of Duccio with her long blue robe and her sleepy Oriental smile keeps a kind of dismantled state, exiled from the high altar of the cathedral in Siena where once she reigned; or if one has mounted to the dusty gallery in San Gimignano where the exquisite madonna of Pinturicchio looks down with shy grace from her quaint mandorla, one may still see a quiet visitor or two apart from "travel" groups. These quiet visitors will be sitting still. They will be looking at the pictures. They will not be putting names, dates, places in a note-book, while they follow their guides at a run. They will not be "getting up" a lecture for the art club. They will not be wondering how many more galleries they ought to see before they connect with the Rome-Paris express. They will not even be reading Howells or Blashfield or Lucas. They will be poised in appreciation of something for its own

Genuine æsthetic experience is usually quiet and slow

142

sake, without any thought of profit or even of utility, as ordinarily understood. If time should stop for them the next moment, it would not cut off an incomplete process. They are not on the way. They are there. They are pausing for a purely æsthetic experience, the emotional enjoyment of beauty for its own sake.

Now such an æsthetic experience depends on the subtle, balanced harmonies which give us at once a sense of a whole. We seize a completed thing, with all its parts fused in a central unity, evident to us in its entirety. When we begin to analyze the parts, or to put special emphasis on the parts, we have already lost the purely æsthetic moment of experience when we were *en rapport* with the whole. For example, we see Duccio's Madonna among her angels against the gorgeous gold background in a unity more complete than separate words can easily indicate. We reach out in single, poised admiration, which is synthetic, not analytic. Later on we may analyze the balance of composition, the blue of the Virgin's long robe, the arrangement of spaces, and so on. Analysis may in turn lead to another moment of pure appreciation, or immediate enjoyment of beauty.

It so happens that the elements of literature are dangerously easy to analyze. They consist of a

143

longer or shorter series of separate words, which even the rapid reader must take in successively. It is not possible to look at the whole at once, as in the case of painting. We can only approximate that effect by concentration in reading, shutting other things out until we have realized our author's conception. All æsthetic experience is individual, and difficult to induce by any deliberate process. It is not strange that teachers of literature have not known how to do it. They have analyzed details in the hope that appreciation would follow, whereas analysis by itself destroys the very mood and quality of appreciation, although it may furnish important facts about a work of art. Appreciation is synthetic.

We have seen that novels not only developed out of many diverse forms, but have taken on accretions of all sorts from science, history, ethics, theology, and other branches of learning. Comparatively few novels have been written purely from the æsthetic point of view. Novels do not stand a comparison in this particular with painting, architecture, sculpture, music, and poetry. Naturally the reader will not so often be called on for the long, slow pause before a thing of beauty when he is reading novels. The subtle, balanced harmonies which make a whole, to be appreciated as a whole, are often lacking in novels. We are more likely to pick out some particular aspect of a novel, whether it be character analysis, or local color, or the presentation of unusual national types. We are more conscious of these particulars than of the whole work of art. We think of the pottery districts of the Five Towns, of the psychopathic personalities of Dostoiefsky, of the Boston that Howells knew, rather than of completed, balanced wholes before which we pause to realize a fine creation, without overemphasis on any one part or aspect. If a novel is a work of art in this sense, characters do not lose their importance, events do not lose their meaning, but they are exquisitely blended into harmonious beauty. We have some novels which may properly be called works of art, although no two critics would agree on quite the same list. Perhaps we may safely include these ten. Others, of course, could be cited.

Eugénie Grandet — Balzac
Under the Greenwood Tree — Hardy
The Scarlet Letter — Hawthorne
A House of Gentlefolk — Turgenev
Un Cœur Simple — Flaubert
The Tale of Genji — Lady Murasaki
Pride and Prejudice — Austen
The Ambassadors — James
Ethan Frome — Wharton
The Bridge of San Luis Rey — Wilder

Balzac, in his *Eugénie Grandet*, achieved the economy of a work of art in which nothing is wasted. He has curbed his tendency to long discussions of agriculture and business, philosophy, metaphysics, morals, and religion. Such details of business as he uses are strictly necessary to the understanding of the miser, Grandet. Descriptions are in perfect harmony with the general theme. Not a word is wasted. Almost with the economy of drama the stage is set in the gloomy stone mansion, a wreck of decayed grandeur, on the steep ascent of the high street of the old town of Saumur. Here Eugénie Grandet, daughter of old Grandet the miser, develops into beauty with provincial simplicity, untouched by her father's schemes, which she does not even comprehend. Formed by her daily work with her mother, and by the village curé, Eugénie's character has innocence without becoming insipid. Perhaps it is her love of beauty which keeps her interesting. She herself is like a fragile flower blooming in a vault. When her cousin Charles comes down in the splendor of a Paris dandy, how should she know that he is a superficial young cad? How indeed? So she walks with him in the mouldy garden, damp under its high walls, and first love was surely never more exquisitely

Eugénie Grandet should be read slowly and evenly

146

portrayed, in so few words. A worm-eaten bench
under an old walnut tree, and lovers saying good-
bye. Why should it be touched with the quality
of lyric poetry? Perhaps because of the contrasts
implied. Cruelty and the lust for power in the
father throw into high relief the one lyric moment
of the daughter. The gay Charles contrasts bril-
liantly with the cold, restrained habits of the starved
household. No wonder that old Nanon, the servant of many years of back-breaking work, cannot
believe that Monsieur Charles really means to wear
his flowered silk dressing gown in his room, when it
ought to furnish an altar for the Virgin, and save
his soul. At length the long tragedy of waiting
ends in disillusion for Eugénie, although nothing
changes the quality of high purity in her being.
She does not become bitter. She is extravagantly
generous with money, to right all her father's wrongs.
She simply goes eternally cold.

Now it is plain from even this rapid summary that
Eugénie Grandet is a harmonious, balanced whole.
The scenes in the high, sombre old town of Saumur
are picturesque, but quite subordinate to the theme.
They have their place exactly in proportion to the
theme, no more, no less. The damp walls and
mouldy paths of the garden have a reminiscence of
ancient grandeur, but only a reminiscence. Con-

sider how Sir Walter Scott might have written several chapters telling us the history of previous owners of such an old fortress in central France. Balzac himself in other novels does something of the sort. But not in *Eugénie Grandet*. The decaying old garden has its importance not as a separate ornament, a piece of bric-a-brac laid on the outside to distract the reader's attention. It is the setting for a brief early love, and its very decay is full of ironic prophecy. Yet the scene is beautiful. Why has it such incredible beauty? We do not know. We only know that the meaning of the whole transfuses all the parts. There is a subtle balance in the whole composition. The same blending of characters can be felt. Eugénie is important, naturally, but she is not over-emphasized. She does not dwarf all the other characters in the book. They all stand out in high relief, yet preserving their exact relations to the whole. Old Nanon, the servant, is worthy of a novel herself. With a shift of emphasis she could become *Un Cœur Simple*, or an *Esther Waters*. Yet a paragraph or two superbly sums up her past. And for her present, how deftly she is introduced, at just the right moments to emphasize Grandet's haggling over the fires and the lights, or her furtive services to her darling Eugénie! Grandet, himself, comes perilously near being a "type" character,

148

but escapes by touches of robust reality in his make-up, and in his long, slow development as a miser. His attempts to play the hearty well-wisher are quite in keeping with his secret hoards. The contrasts between the resignation of the humbled wife and mother and the gay frivolity of Charles add color for a moment. On the whole, however, the tones are sombre.

How shall we read this book? Obviously we shall not read it with our finger tips turning the pages while we are at lunch. We shall not skip here and there looking for the high spots. A trained skipper may retire before *Eugénie Grandet* and give up his art, unless he wishes to lose something blended so intimately with the whole that he is losing the whole. In quiet, in peace, somewhere with no distractions should the reader approach a masterpiece of art such as this. It will not do to carry in the subway. Furthermore, one should deliberately slow down the reading to an even, regular pace which will take all parts of the book about equally. It should be the equivalent of looking at a painting or a cathedral arch. Since this type of purely appreciative reading does not call for pauses to analyze problems, it will be possible to secure an effect of unity in the reading. *Eugénie Grandet* is not long. Several very quiet hours should be enough. The pace should be steady, unhurried, even. The reading is easy in one sense, since its art makes it seem easy. The thing moves with the quiet inevitability of murmuring brooks, or surf. It is not complicated with questions or problems, and to insert them would be impertinent intrusion. Problems are not roused in the reader's mind, as they are by many contemporary novels. Therefore the actual time consumed will not be great. The attitude of slow, quiet enjoyment is what counts. We shall hardly find ourselves lingering over definite passages for their particular beauty, since their beauty is so intimately woven into the whole.

If we look at the full title of Thomas Hardy's *Under the Greenwood Tree*, we shall find a very useful hint for the reading of it. In full, the

Under the Greenwood Tree should be read slowly

title is *Under the Greenwood Tree, or The Mellstock Quire, A Rural Painting of the Dutch School.* Hardy himself indicates here exactly the attitude to be taken toward his rural characters of Mellstock-Lane. They are like figures in a genre painting of the Dutch school. The details of homely Dutch interiors come to mind. Although the villagers of Mellstock are English to the backbone, yet the rustic scenes are quite in the realistic Dutch manner and have the same curious blending of the

absurd with the comic-grotesque. The same poignant quality deepens the realism. One thinks of the
old Dutch woman, still strong and capable at her
wheel, yet wrinkling her face in the attempt to
thread her needle. Just so old William Dewy in
Hardy's novel must give up playing his bass-viol
in the choir which he has served since he was eleven.
It is an additional touch of Hardy's irony that the
stringed instruments give way to the new craze for
the whining church organ. The reader knows, with
scarcely a direct word from the author to tell him
so, that the old carols sung to the violins by the
village singers on a frosty Christmas eve are far
more quaintly musical than the hymns droned to
a wheezy village organ. The contrast puts a sudden depth of dignity into old Dewy's resignation.
It is poignant. For the rest, the rich details can
often be grotesquely funny. The dancing on the
sanded floor, the motley costumes, the varieties of
home brew, the Western dialect, the shoemaker's
house with the low shop-window framing the portrait of Mr. Penny at work with his awl and, finally,
the wedding dances under the greenwood tree, all
blend together in a finely wrought genre painting
in literature.

To hurry the reading of it, or to skip passages,
would be simply to miss the essential quality.

151

True, there is plenty of joviality in many scenes, such as the ridiculous questioning of Thomas Leaf, the village fool who could not be spared from the choir because his high treble could reach upper G. The absurdity may carry some scenes along more swiftly for the reader than a sombre or tragic quality would carry them. In general, a fairly even pace will be best, as we pause long enough to take one rich bit of country life after another, — little vignettes, pictures rather than stories. There are again no problems to delay us. We can carry our even, steady reading through to the end. This is the only equivalent in literary appreciation for looking quietly at a painting.

The Scarlet Letter affords an excellent chance to make fine distinctions in reading. Here is a novel so æsthetic in purpose, mode, and treatment that its revolutionary discussions of a woman's problems passed almost unnoticed in the New England of 1850. They are completely subordinated to the vivid interplay of the story and its mystical scarlet symbol. The analysis of Dimmesdale's secret mental tortures, along with Hester's release through open confession, proceeds in such conformity to modern psychology that it could be used as illustrative material. Fortunately Hawthorne

The Scarlet Letter should be first absorbed as a work of art

did not know the words "complex", "repression", "psychopathic." Nor would it have occurred to him to speak of Hester's "sex drive." Therefore the material is covered with a matchless delicacy which never becomes prudish. Moreover, it is so well proportioned that it never attracts notice. It simply glides into the subtle undercurrents of the book. *The Scarlet Letter* has even entered the American schools, with only an uneasy suspicion now and then on the part of some village principal who could not find any one passage showing Hester as actually sorry for what she did. Most readers have never looked for such a passage until recent critics have pointed out that there is none. Far from it. Sheer artistic quality has carried a book of 1850 whose fundamental thought is radical to-day. Are not the readers of eighty years right in their emphasis? Should it not be read first of all as an æsthetic experience? Let us absorb its beauty as one magnificent scene follows another, colored with the richness of the stained glass in Chartres cathedral, yet never too ornate with detail. Something like this should be our first impression. An even rate, unhurried, yet somewhat more fluent and rapid than the one we use for contemplative reading will enable us to seize the whole in its noble entirety. There should be practically no pauses. Afterwards,

153

however, the analysis of points of view and implied beliefs should be made in another reading. We shall consider this matter of re-reading in a later section.

Notable critics, such as Henry James, Howells, Flaubert, and others, have admired Turgenev's art as almost peerless. Certainly in the adaptation of means to ends, in the rigid economy of styles, he probably has no equal. He gains his effects in the fewest possible words, after merciless excision of unimportant detail. Consequently his limpid simplicity of manner is like the surface of a quiet pool with unsounded depths. It can easily throw us off our guard, and deceive us into taking one of our more rapid paces in reading. The reader who is thus beguiled will miss the depth of Turgenev. Sometimes a portrait is condensed into a single sentence which not only brings a character before us, but implies a profound observation and analysis. Sometimes a single sentence is packed with the history of years. Not only the minor characters in the ordinary sense, but the mere chance figures of a scene are so highly individualized in a few words that it will not do to assume the house servants any more than the village peasants, the great-aunts any more than the stray tutor. We shall miss some priceless, peculiar beauty if we do. Old Anton, in

Turgenev's House of Gentlefolk should be read very slowly

154

A House of Gentlefolk, — bowing to the ground and kissing his master's hand, calling his master "Little Father" while he relates old family tales for his amusement, taking a humble place in the bare courtyard to sleep, — is only one example of the old Russian servant so close to the serf era. We know his whole life of slavish devotion in a paragraph or so.

We come upon an old canopy bedstead with faded cushions and see at its head the picture of the "Holy Mother of God; it was the very picture which the old maid, dying alone and forgotten by every one, had for the last time pressed to her chilling lips." Are not the repressions of a whole life-time implied here in this superb sentence? Do we need seven chapters of amateur psychoanalysis in the manner of the ordinary modern novel? But how easily the few significant words could be missed in the midst of a seemingly casual paragraph about an old manor house! The music master, too, a mere minor figure, is etched in a few incomparable strokes to show his genuine gifts, lost in shy, embittered futility. Even the moments which would ordinarily be preparatory or casual in a novel represent some unusual impression of life, something which we all recognize at once as familiar, and yet strange on the printed page. It is as if a secret experience peculiar to ourselves sud-

denly leapt at us from the text, with an added poignant beauty. The dreamy silences of the country,
for instance, with the noiseless flight of swallows
overhead, and the sense of nameless expectancy
while time slips by like water in the marshlands
unobserved. What is it we expect? Why are we
suddenly a little sad when the swallows fly noise-
lessly? Why, indeed? We do not know. We only
know that Turgenev has seized a quality of feeling,
unique in words, and yet overwhelmingly real in
human experience.

Nevertheless, *A House of Gentlefolk* is not delayed
by any problems nor difficult questions, even con-
cerning character. All is clearness itself. But we
shall surely miss the depths of it if we do not
read at our slow, even rate, whatever that rate may
be for the particular individual concerned. Elisa-
veta, or Lisa, as she is called, has a certain resem-
blance to Eugénie Grandet in her provincial innocence which never becomes insipidity. The tragic
irony of Lisa's love is greater than that of Eugénie's.
The reader always knows that Charles would have
disappointed Eugénie in any case. Marriage with
him would probably have given her a greater dis-
illusionment than the one she suffered. Therefore
we are more willing to accept the wintry purity of
her charities at the end. The reader of *A House*

of Gentlefolk can never forget that Lavretsky was essentially all that Lisa dreamed of, in nobility, in fine feeling, and in a romantic passion deepened by his previous sufferings. It was her provincial religious training, already stiffening into rigidity, which surrounded her with a mist through which she could but dimly perceive his sad, yet ardent manliness. Hence the tragedy was greater because it was unnecessary, at least from our point of view to-day, and probably also from Turgenev's point of view, although he is too great an artist to remark upon it. No banalities accompany his theme. He simply tells us very quietly what happened. All is just as it had to be; and if we wish to pull out of his text an argument for divorce, or greater freedom, or less rigid training, it will be our doing, not his. A very child's tale could not be freer of such matters than his.

Lavretsky himself does not argue with Lisa. He accepts, when he knows he must. And after all, what a fascinating quality Lisa's purity has! Her grave eyes, regarding Lavretsky with simple amazement when he asks her why she goes to church; her quiet acceptance of his instant apology, and his request that she pray for him; her enjoyment of out-of-door pleasures in her white frock with its wide white sash and her large beribboned hat all belong to the vanished heroine. Yet she does not resemble Thackeray's Amelia Sedley, nor any other Victorian maiden. Lisa's poetic depths of feeling keep her from insipidity, even though she retreats in terror from those depths to her final escape in the cloister. The extraordinary closing lines are saved from sad futility by the suggestion of rich, poignant depths of experience below sorrow itself. Lavretsky visited the remote convent and saw Lisa once. "Crossing over from choir to choir, she walked close past him, moving with the even, hurried, but meek walk of a nun; and she did not glance at him; only the eyelashes on the side towards him quivered a little, only she bent her emaciated face lower, and the fingers of her clasped hands entwined with her rosary were pressed still closer to one another. What were they both thinking, what were they feeling? Who can know? Who can say? There are such moments in life, there are such feelings. . . . One can but point to them . . . and pass them by."

The noble *andante* movement of these closing words of the novel is evident in the excellent translation of Constance Garnett. The words are simple, and very easy to follow. But they suggest the profundities of life and death, separation, temperament, belief, the richness of years, of loss, of faith, of devotion in futility, of mysterious poignant fulfillment

158

in pain. Clumsy explanations cannot convey them. They must be felt, they must be heard by the quiet, inward ear. To hurry the reading would be like putting Beethoven's Ninth Symphony to the speed rhythm of the subway express. Rather should we take the longest of winter evenings, broken only by the tapping of snowflakes on the pane, and the falling log in the fireplace. If we read *A House of Gentlefolk* through in such a long evening, with nothing to break the impression, and yet with nothing to hurry us, we shall store up for ourselves one of the memories that, as Wordsworth said of Nature, can never betray us.

Turgenev and Flaubert were personal friends, discussing often the principles of art which they held in common. It will not surprise us, therefore, to find in Flaubert's work much the same kind of æsthetic quality and emphasis. There is, however, a keen edge of social satire in Flaubert which makes a less purely æsthetic appeal. In one of his shorter novels, *Un Cœur Simple*, — properly a long tale rather than a novel, — he has etched the portrait of an old family servant in memorable beauty, the more remarkable for the unpromising nature of the subject. The old woman has never had a single experience of ordinary interest. Life is drenched for her in humdrum menial service. No

Un Cœur Simple should be read in the original if possible

blackguard gentlemen woo her or frighten her into fainting as pretty Pamela is frightened. No dainty caps, no black silk aprons, no frilled tuckers make her piquant. She is just the old drudge. Yet the portrait is exquisitely beautiful in unconscious humility and naïve devotion. Even when her days of usefulness are over, and she is dying, forgotten in her attic, merciful delirium keeps her from sordid misery, while she lives over the happy moments when she dressed her little charges in white veils for their first communion. Here the French is so exquisite that we shall miss a great deal of the quality if we do not read it in the original. And reading in the original means, for most English readers, a slower rate.

The æsthetic novel is not always linked with a tragic mood. The delicate touches of Lady Murasaki's *Tale of Genji* are light and joyous like fairies' wings, or figures on a dainty screen where firelight plays. Perhaps it is partly the exotic flavor of this old, courtly, romantic satire of Japan which makes the western reader refuse to take even its pathetic moments seriously. There is a delightful unreality about virtues, vices, heroines, ladies, princes, and princesses therein. Nevertheless, if we should skim it lightly, as a fairy

The Tale of Genji by Lady Murasaki needs slow reading without much analysis

tale, we should lose some of its exotic beauties, its flowers of old Japan. We need to read quietly, slowly, yet not analytically, as we absorb a work of marvelous art into our lives. The fourth and final volume of *The Tale of Genji*, called *Blue Trousers*, needs very careful reading, without pauses or cross-references.

Many critics might question the use of Jane Austen's novels primarily for the æsthetic approach. They are incomparable studies of late eighteenth-century manners, as well as of **Jane** character. They could be used for so- **Austen's** ciological and psychological data. But *Pride and* the delicate balance of interests, the lumi- **Prejudice** nous yet quiet wit of the dialogues, the nice **should be absorbed** adjustment of characters to one another, **first of all** without undue emphasis on any individ- **as a work** ual, suggest rather the æsthetic approach. **of art** Certainly that should be the first approach. We should read straight ahead to get the story in all its exquisite proportions as a complete whole, although we may mark a passage or so here and there for re-reading and later emphasis. Mr. Bennet's wit, Mr. Collins's ridiculous proposals, Mrs. Bennet's vulgar blunders, Elizabeth's high-spirited duels with Mr. Darcy, all need pauses and re-reading, as we shall see in a later section. But the book should be

161

grasped as a whole, complete in all its parts, with no omissions whatever, and in a steady, even rate of reading, not a fast rate, but with few or no pauses. It could be taken in a sitting of from four and one half to six and one half hours, as we have found by experiment.

The Ambassadors is one of the best novels of the middle period of Henry James. It is difficult reading, necessitating a comparatively slow rate if it is to be followed in all its subtle implications. If it were more simple, however, it would still need a slow, long reading. Our students have found Henry James very difficult. The frequent halting interruptions of his thought do not suggest the inevitability of art. Furthermore, they irritate the reader, who feels justified in revolting at some excessively subtle modification of a statement, before the statement itself is given with clarity. The subtle modification would be evident in the course of the action without so many obvious halts. Nevertheless, we have in *The Ambassadors* an extremely delicate work of art, worth the pains of grasping in its entirety.

The Ambassadors needs very careful reading

Consider for a moment the rarefied theme. A son of New England, from Woollett, Massachusetts, has been caught by the fascinations of Paris and

162

particularly of a French woman. The combination spells vague orgies of ruin to the Woollett imagination, in the days before a trip to Paris was a casual thing. Chad Newsome has long outstayed the period of respectable sojourn in France. He must be rescued from the toils of the charmer, and return to active life in Woollett. Hence one ambassador after another goes to Paris to reclaim the youth. Lambert Strether is the first, and it is through his eyes that we see all the rest. He finds Chad Newsome with a cosmopolitan cultivation unknown in Woollett, Massachusetts. He finds that the dreaded French woman, Madame de Vionnet, has not only made Chad over, but has in herself rich depths of power, æsthetic development, subtle varieties of feeling, of knowledge, of beauty, that reveal mercilessly to Lambert Strether all that he has failed to attain in life, all that he is just too late to attain — including the Countess. That poignant mood of appreciation mingled with regret seizes him, dominates him throughout the story. He catches the glamor of life among old things of beauty. At last he hesitates in his ambassadorship. Shall he bring Chad back to Woollett? Rather his efforts change to a determination to keep him in Paris, if possible. Meantime his cooling letters rouse fear at home, and the Pococks are sent out to the rescue. In a scene of delicate contrasts we have Sarah Pocock boasting that she "*knows* Paris" when Madame de Vionnet offers the services of a French countess! We have the crudities of prosperous America mercilessly placed beside the product of centuries of social training. At last the ambassadors all retire, Strether leaving a situation fraught with coming tragedy for Madame de Vionnet. The reader sees clearly enough that she will lose Chad Newsome in the end, because he is not quite fine enough for the situation; that she has begun to appreciate Strether; that the last scene between the Countess and Strether in the long, formal drawing room with the gleam of candles on the polished floor is full of regret for them both, and with no banal consolations. Lambert Strether plays the game. He has deliberately thrown up his ambassadorship, but he will take nothing for himself.

Such a brief account will show at least the balanced completeness of the central conception. It is not emphasized in any one part or aspect more than in the others. It does not require long pauses for analysis, cross-references, and comparisons between one page and another in the book. The ultimate connections are all clear when we have mastered the difficult individual sentences one by one. The Pocks, Strether, Chad Newsome, the Countess fall into their places in the scheme, with no special

164

emphasis on any one development, although in general we see the situation through Strether's eyes. Slowly we shall appreciate the fine scenes. There are ironies to meditate upon, but not to delay the reader with analysis and comparison in order to understand. Reading James is a kind of habit that grows easier with time and practice. We learn to discount the parentheses with less annoyance, as we become accustomed to his minute distinctions of mood and tense. We know the Jamesian turn of expression, and can sift out his essential meaning more quickly. One help is to concentrate on his main clauses at first, letting his qualifications go until we have seized the principal statement in a sentence. Thus we shall gradually become accustomed to his tortuous, indirect style.

Mrs. Wharton's *Ethan Frome* affords a contrast in clarity and in elimination. Every irrelevant subtlety is gone, and the story stands bleak and bare as Starkfield itself, lost in its snowdrifts through the winter. *Ethan Frome* could be read rapidly so far as general comprehension is concerned. But the descriptions, like etchings in black and white, might be unduly slurred. They draw the clear-cut, merciless lines of Ethan's surroundings as if they were a part of his fate. His gaunt, square

Ethan Frome is a highly concentrated work of art

165

house against the snows of the New England hills is off the main road and isolated, like Ethan himself. It will not do to lose any of these implications in a too swift reading. We must flounder with Ethan's old horse in those snowdrifts. We must feel the icy breath in the unheated rooms of that house, and the contrast in the one warm central kitchen. We must watch Ethan's anguished struggle to escape. We must give an unhurried appreciation to the ironic futility of his outlived dream. No close analysis will be needed. It all stands clear, with the inevitability of a Greek tragedy, to be quietly felt as a whole. Ethan is so clearly one of the promising half-way men, paralyzed by the niggardly life he is born to, that his character needs no special study. The two women are also clear to us at once. The reading should be an appreciative æsthetic experience, taking the object as a whole without dissection or analysis.

It is gratifying to include a recent American book in our list of ten. Thornton Wilder's *Bridge of San Luis Rey* is compressed until it seems a meagre outline, judged by ordinary narrative standards, yet seldom have the major characters in a novel stood forth with more satisfying and intense reality. They are there in the round, instead of as the flat

The Bridge of San Luis Rey should be read slowly

patterns or abstractions which we might expect from such brief sketching. Even the environment of old Peru is startlingly clear, because every phrase is packed with rich allusions or allusive quality. Yet the compression never makes the style obscure. The characters are unusual, with subtle changes and overtones, but they are never difficult. In all this rigid economy we are yet fully aware of their whole lives, their essential ambitions, their dreams, their sufferings, their inhibitions, their vices, their obsessions, their sacrifices. The drunken old Marquesa de Montemayor with her hopeless dream is no less real than the abbess with her long plans to which she will sacrifice individuals. Above all, it is the tragic juxtaposition of these characters which makes it important to see them in their ironic contrasts all at once, with no dissection nor analysis, but with a full, long, slow, quiet look of genuine appreciation.

Æsthetic experience, then, is what these masterpieces of art in fiction should give us. **Why are** One significant fact will be noted about **the great-** **est novels** the list, or about any similar list. The **not** masterpieces of art in fiction are there, **among** but the greatest novels of the world will **the** **master-** surely not be. How shall we explain such **pieces of** a seeming contradiction in terms ? Simply **art?** by recalling that the novel is not a pure art form,

167

but a kind of hybrid, only now and then forced into balanced form and exquisite proportions by some artist like Hardy or Turgenev or Hawthorne. If, on the other hand, we were to make a list of ten great novels as ordinarily understood, would not the list be something like this?

Don Quixote — Cervantes
Tom Jones — Fielding
The Brothers Karamazoff — Dostoiefsky
Vanity Fair — Thackeray
David Copperfield — Dickens
Les Misérables — Victor Hugo
Jerusalem — Lagerlöf
Growth of the Soil — Hamsun
Fathers and Sons — Turgenev
Roderick Random — Smollett

Lacking balance and proportion in some respects, these would be admitted by all critics into the front rank of the great novels of the world. Why? Because they convey characters with a superb, epic range. And just here we touch the peculiar excellence of the novel at its best. Developed from many diverse forms, it has acquired a flexibility peculiarly suited to the elaboration of fine shades of personality, delicate nuances that would be lost in the high lights of the theatre, and that do not belong to the rhythms of poetry, even of free verse. They require careful development in clear prose, unhindered and unhurried by the need of compression in stricter art forms. The novelist has time to tell us fully not only what his characters do and say, but what they think, what he thinks about them, what all the other characters think about them, and finally how they seem to the world at large, judged by the standards of their day. Furthermore, a novelist like Arnold Bennett, Galsworthy, Turgenev, or Balzac is a highly sensitized instrument for receiving experience, and for conveying it to us. This experience is not necessarily his own but is often derived from his intense observation of the characters he meets and perhaps fuses together. Along with his observation goes a sympathetic understanding of such depth that he can place himself in the very crises through which his imagined personalities are passing. He realizes them vividly, as he writes. It is because he has transmuted his actual observation into his portraits that they become studies of personality which make the ordinary "case studies" of the social worker seem thin and superficial. For the great novelist has more depth of understanding, more vivid imagination. He identifies himself with his characters. He is there through the interminable night with Clayhanger, watching by his father's bed. And

169

the author is also struggling for breath on that bed with the dying old man.

These facts are beginning to be recognized by psychologists who use the characters in novels for studies of varied types in social contacts. Many difficult traits of personality have been analyzed first in novels. Without any scientific nomenclature, with only the vocabulary of the usual human interchange, novelists of power have traced every subtle shade of feeling before it becomes dynamic in action, or inaction, on the part of the characters. Especially in recent years the genuine interest in major and minor deviations of behavior has been registered in a remarkable series of portraits in contemporary fiction.

The novel is an excellent vehicle for varied traits of personality

Here we come to actual problems of character in our reading of novels. What general differences of approach will be needed? Instead of quiet absorption in the purely æsthetic appreciation of a balanced, harmonious whole, without the intrusion of problems, there will now be thought-provoking questions to consider. We have reached the points to be sharply and deliberately challenged. The novelist's account of motives in the subtle changes of the character-novel should lead to slower rates and pauses for thought. Yet it is in reading these great character-novels, often so uneven in their quality, that our students have found the best opportunities to change their rates most swiftly and profitably, and at length develop a whole gamut of flexible reading skills, to be turned on or off at will.

In Chapter IV we saw that many fine novels have inferior passages, repetitions, interludes, and digressions, to be boldly skipped or skimmed. In the development of the important characters, on the other hand, there is an excellent chance to slow down at once, in the manner of the late President Harper, who could change his rate in an instant, from devouring speed to close scrutiny of the individual words, even to the thoughtful pause for new or difficult matter. Our best students, after some practice, learn to take from eight to ten different rates as they handle these novels. They will skip or skim the irrelevant by-paths, read the ordinary course of events with varying moderate to fast rates, and then pause to note some important questions of character either along the margin of the book or in their note-books. Especially they note any statement by the author of the fundamental theme or idea of the book, or of special significance of character. In all this we are very near to study-rates of reading. Yet we have skipped perhaps three or four chapters of the same novel.

For example, Scott's *Heart of Midlothian* affords a fine opportunity for discrimination and variety in reading rates. The general reader will be quite justified in skipping the introductory epistle, the introduction, the postscript to the introduction, the preliminary chapter, and the first three chapters, since they give detailed historical accounts of Scottish antiquities or of events very loosely connected with the story. With chapter four, we can begin reading for the general flavor of Scotch life, and for a slender thread of story, but we should read cursorily, skimming over much irrelevant matter at our fastest rate. With chapter eight, we can at last plunge into the story. It is the ordinary melodramatic tale until chapter eleven, and we should go at a rapid pace, although not too fast to seize the connections of the story. In chapter eleven, there is a great deal of learned religious discussion with Latin terms which may be skipped with a glance by the general reader, simply to get the purport.

Resuming a rapid reading pace, we should press on to chapter thirteen, where the interest of the tale broadens and deepens with Jeanie's problem. Here, although the dramatic quality increases, the reader should slow down to a moderate rate for the understanding of Jeanie Deans, her attitude at her sister's trial, and her preparations for the long journey on foot to London. With chapter twenty-six we should follow Jeanie on her journey without missing a single piquant detail of the rich character study, even pausing over her quaint letters written on the road, with their practical sympathy and their unconscious charm. We follow the simple peasant as she puts on shoes and stockings every day after entering England, although she fears that they will think her extravagant at home.

Finally, in chapter thirty-six, when she pleads before the Queen in London for her sister's life, we should re-read that eloquent passage for its beauty and simplicity. It will be well to note down the lines showing Jeanie's traits of character throughout this section up to chapter forty-one. The last ten chapters, however, form an anti-climax to the great story, and can be skimmed rapidly to the conclusion. Thus we can with great profit actually change our reading rate nine times in reading this famous novel of character, because it is so uneven in quality.

No such practice ground for the break-up of fixed rates of reading, and for the productive use of flexible changing rates can be found in all literature as the novel of character, with its frequent uneven qualities suggesting these changes in rate.

Furthermore, the reader should actually pause to sum up his questions, and especially for cross-comparisons with similar characters either in fiction or in life. Where has he known a personality like the one analyzed before him on the page? In some other novel of the same author? In some novel of a different author? In life itself? He will thus gradually accumulate significant groups of similar characters with subtle distinctions to analyze and to understand. He will become skilled in relating new figures in fiction to their counterparts at once. Breadth and scope in understanding human life the sure to result.

Let us consider a few typical character groupings of this sort. Take the not infrequent case of simple incompleteness. It is not failure, as ordinarily understood, still less wrongdoing, under any social code. Yet there is something tragically inadequate about the individual. He is commonly enough met. He is one of the "almost men", who never arrive. Yet what a depth of insight some novelists have shown in handling this ordinary fact! We understand more fully the qualities which leave a personality stranded in tragic incompleteness after we read Galsworthy's *Fraternity*. Here the crux of the trouble seems to lie in the temperament itself, in something not to be cured by circumstance. Probably it goes back to early influences, although

Personalities of tragic incompleteness

174

the relations between heredity and environment are not yet soundly enough established for certainty on this point. In any case, the traits of such an individual are of long standing, and seem basic, unalterable, constantly recurring in action or inaction. Hilary Dallison, in Galsworthy's *Fraternity*, has retired into a hyperæsthesia rendering him incapable of positive living, in spite of a fine mentality. He is not even capable of wrong-doing when once he smells the stale violet powder on the little model. Repulsion takes him back into his class again, and into passivity. We see a fine analytical, reflective mind preying upon itself, perpetually, never fulfilling itself in any adequate way.

Another excellent example occurs in Pirandello's *The Late Mattia Pascal*. Here the brilliant novelist has found a peculiar situation for his study of temperament. He lets his weak character have a new chance at life. Mattia unexpectedly finds that he is regarded as dead, as "the late Mattia Pascal" in his Italian village. He has money in his pocket. He may go where he will. He may name himself what he will. He is like a personage in a fairy tale with unlimited power. His creator has let him be born again, only he has the opportunity to profit by past mistakes, since he keeps his own inward identity. What happens? Within a short time he is caught in a situation very like his former life. He knows no way to meet it but escape. He is bullied by the same fears, the same longings, the same sense of inadequacy. He is just "the late Mattia Pascal" again, with the same temperamental weaknesses, emphasized by his new chance in life, which could no nothing for him.

Other examples of the same difficulty will occur to every reader. A study of pessimism, apparently incurable, has been made by the Spanish novelist Pio Baroja in *The Tree of Knowledge*, with a sensitive, finely endowed hero, Andres Hurtado, who cannot conquer his despair over the corruptions in politics and the ironies of life. The subtle forces of psychological maladjustment in Marcel Prévost's fine novel *His Mistress and I* play themselves out in a drama no less tense because the changes from day to day are chiefly those of inward feeling. The entire situation is characteristically French, with its lucidity and its inevitability. Given these characters and they will be tormented with just such misunderstandings. Antoine cannot help torturing himself with doubts, and the more he doubts, the more Sophie realizes that he is not the man to hold her mind. In the end he holds nothing. Tragic mistakes in character mean loss and unfulfillment. Anne Parrish has analyzed the unfulfillment of

176

arrested lives in *The Perennial Bachelor* with admirable detail. Here we do not feel the tragedy to be quite so much inherent in the characters as in the circumstances of early childhood and youth. But the results are just as inescapable.

Especially clear instances of tragic incompleteness appear in Russian fiction. Social repressions of centuries could easily result in many types of passivity, ready for the novelist's observation. How familiar in the pages of Dostoiefsky and of Turgenev is the eloquent liberal who gathers a little coterie of followers about him to discuss the salvation of Russia, often behind closed doors! Books are projected, pamphlets written, meetings proposed, usually for "next year." Sometimes he retires to the country as a tutor or guide on one of the large rural manors of the nobility in Central Russia. Stepan Trofimovitch Verhovensky, for example, becomes a sort of retainer on the estate of Varvara Petrovna, in Dostoiefsky's novel, *The Possessed.* Long after his nominal duties as tutor are over, Stepan remains on the estate, still talking eloquently of the books he will write, of the emancipation of Russia, while he consumes more and more vodka with his cronies, and becomes a more arrant coward each year. The analysis is painstakingly exact, extending to the very roots of his inaction in fear. Nikolay Stavrogin, the heir of the estate, has no such fears as those which beset his old tutor. Nevertheless, his is just as truly and much more tragically a case of unfulfillment. He has no outlets for his violent energies, which take their revenge in extravagances of abasement and generosity ending in suicide. Stavrogin is a marvellous clinical study of marked deviations, accompanying brilliant mental abilities.

Fiction has a charming gallery of beggars, "ne'er-do-weels", prodigals, and rogues. Ranging all the **Beggars** way from the picaresque escapades of **and** Lazarillo de Tormes to Huckleberry Finn **"ne'er-** on his raft, and including such varied **do-weels"** **in fiction** figures as Du Bose Heyward's Porgy, with the immemorial wisdom of his Oriental passivity in the fine art of his begging, and Rip van Winkle, the amiable old drunkard of the Catskills, these reprobates are uniformly lovable. Seldom doing actual harm, taking their problems lightly, for the most part, they belong to the carefree vagabondage no longer possible to humanity at large. Is it not perhaps just because they remind us of the former days in the woods and on the open sea, in the wilder life to which we all secretly long to escape, that we find these rogues enchanting? We can escape vicariously with them for a time, playing at magic dreams with Rip in the mountains, and watching for the shores of the dark Mississippi at dawn with Huck. These are vagabonds that we know and understand instinctively. Very little detail suffices, and yet novelists have analyzed the types with exhaustive care. The lack of responsibility comes out in many forms. The causes are various, and often explained with great care. The main fact, however, is always clear. For one reason or another, these rogues have escaped from civilized duties, civilized forms, civilized customs, civilized relations. They are a law unto themselves. They may often be hungry and cold, but they are never cramped. Towards them we have a perennial indulgence.

In striking contrast to these vagabonds, a group of sturdy laborers may be observed in fiction. They are hard workers with strong, soiled hands, whether blackened at the forge, like Joe Gargery's, or soiled from wielding the hammer, like Adam Bede's, or blistered in the Nordland cold like Isak's, in Hamsun's *Growth of the Soil*, or roughened at the churn like Jeanie Deans's. Certain marked differences might appear on close analysis between city and country toilers, village and field workers, but on the whole the likenesses outweigh the differences. A peculiar solidity characterizes them one and all, an enviable slow sanity, as if the earth herself had rewarded them for their

Rural and urban laborers in fiction

179

closeness to her. Their feet are solidly poised on the ground. The work of their hands is as good, honest, dependable as their word. They do not fly off in revolts or rages or escapes. Day by day, hour by hour, they are piling up the useful products of their toil, with long, sustained, steady resistance to the forces of idleness and despair. They accept the burdens of civilized life without regarding themselves as heroic. Indeed, perhaps their finest quality is their lack of heroics. They do not pose in self-pity. They do not spend anguished nights in despair or repentance. Their sleep is long, sweet, and unbroken. If they rise to eloquence, in rare moments, like Jeanie Deans before her Queen, they are the last ones to know it. In simplicity and unconsciousness Jeanie can turn in the next hour to her Highland cheeses, without a trace of an idea that the long walk from Edinburgh to London has made a heroine of an unprotected girl in the eighteenth century. Small wonder that modern psychiatry is attempting cures by hard labor. The one defect in these workers is the lack of imaginative range and understanding of life.

Their slowness must not be confused with actual mental inferiority. Adam Bede and Joe Gargery can deal with any crisis nobly and effectually once they perceive it. They are simply slower than the highly developed

"Inno-cents" in fiction

artist or intellectual. We have also in fiction an extraordinary group of characters showing marked mental deficiencies, rendering them in greater or less degree unable to handle the affairs of life, yet with uncanny, piercing, intuitive understanding, sometimes united with finer feelings than those of the clever manipulators of events. Here is an aspect of character well worth study in novels. Prince Myshkin, for example, in Dostoiesfky's *Idiot*, is a beggar and an infant in both financial and social adjustments. The crises of life leave him finally shattered in hopeless idiocy. Events which a clever intelligence would have foreseen and averted break over his helplessness unmitigated by any intervention of mercy for his condition. Every one about him assumes that he can deal with life at first hand, although his epilepsy alone should have indicated special care. Yet this prince with the mind of a child has an insight that can startle clever rogues. He knows their intentions, whether of murder or theft, although he cannot prevent them. His knowledge would be in many instances valuable to the authorities, since it is far ahead of any other information, and it is uniformly accurate. Even if only used for its indications, its probabilities, it would afford excellent basis for analysis and subsequent judgment. Furthermore, Prince Myshkin has the mystic's sense of the highest human values, so that in his society there is a marked elevation of tone. All these traits are hopelessly broken down.

Selma Lagerlöf has given us an even clearer portrait of a similar character in *The Emperor of Portugallia*. Jan of Ruffluck Croft is drawn with amazing skill, and without a word of ordinary psychological analysis. Yet the imperceptible stages of his delusion are so exactly indicated that they would form excellent material for a close study of psychiatric disturbance. Jan cannot bear the knowledge that his daughter has gone astray in the city. His little girl, whom he named Glory Goldie Sunnycastle after the sun, must be a great empress afar off somewhere, who will come back to astonish them all in time. The delusion is aptly called in simple village talk, a shade which our Lord has put before his eyes that he may not see what he could not bear. This is very exact. Delusions are often a smoke screen to save the individual from the truth. Now note the interesting development of Jan's intuitive power. Partly because he has a natural depth of feeling, partly because of the superstitions of the village about "innocents", and partly from mere chance Jan acquires a reputation for supernatural insight. The reputation increases his confidence in himself. We have at length a kind of village seer, regarded with

182

awe mingled with familiar knowledge of Jan's mental defect. The judgment of the village comes very near to accuracy in the main points, moreover, although some details show merely the superstitions of the villages. The life on his tiny croft, or farm, with the kindly understanding of simple folk, keeps Jan from serious extremes until the end. One curious fact must be carefully noted by the student of character. Jan really knows all the time what has become of Goldie. When he describes the wicked enemies pursuing the empress, he mentions well-known sins. Probably some dim allegory of the regal soul beset by spiritual foes had captured his imagination along with the far-off Portugallia, — a name to him, nothing more. The ability thus to deceive ourselves with pretty stories seems well-nigh endless, and can be studied in novels to great advantage.

Other examples will occur to the reader. There is, of course, Jacob Wasserman's recent treatment of the legend of Caspar Hauser, the mysterious lad, partly feebleminded yet with gleams of genius. On a higher social and intellectual level, what is Colonel Newcome but a child in the affairs of ordinary society, even though he is one of the most lovable characters in all fiction? Bear in mind that he can handle the routine duties of his post in the army in

India with admirable accuracy and the unquestioned honor of an English officer. The life in the barracks, the stated pay, the simple round of hours leave him time to dream of his return to England, and his reunion with the boy for whom he has lived. He sees himself an honored retired Colonel, living in ample comfort with his son, and helping that son to see a little of the world before settling down to a profession. The dream is partially realized. But how soon the Colonel shows that he is unable to cope with the complications of cosmopolitan London life! His difficulty in understanding rogues and snobs comes from his very fineness of feeling. Not having Prince Myshkin's clairvoyant mystical quality, the Colonel judges others by his own standards. He cannot imagine that anyone ever lies. Lying is foreign to an officer and a gentleman. So he becomes the prey of bank swindlers. He cannot imagine a guest insulting his host with a leer of ridicule. So his son, who has really been right in resenting the mockery of his father, must be hauled out of bed betimes to apologize to the cad. The Colonel's quixotic humility may endear him to some of us extravagantly, but he fails to understand the obvious traits of those meaner than himself, when he allows himself to be openly mocked at his own dinner, and then assumes that he must have been ridiculous enough to merit it. Yet, withal, he is never over-sensitive. Open-heartedly he throws money and gifts and favors about him, until at length the awakening leaves him dazed. He bows his white head in humility that is now helpless before the storm of vulgar abuse. A child in the affairs of the world, yes, a failure, if you like, but the finest gentleman of all fiction as he stands among the charity almoners, — the old men of Grey Friars.

A pertinent social question arises very naturally from the study of such characters. Shall we ever learn to protect them from the contacts which are too difficult for them, in order that their rare abilities, qualities, and fine discernments may be of use along their own lines? Shall we forbid their being shattered by too heavy strains, or beggared by financial problems which they cannot handle? Is there any way of saving them? Students enjoy discussing the question, especially if they can bring any knowledge of sociology to the discussion.

As we ascend the scale from the "innocents" in fiction, we shall come upon those famous idealists, first and foremost of whom stands Don Quixote with his quaint mistakes. A scullery wench can be a princess in an instant of his imagination, a wretched inn can be a castle, and a windmill can be a dragon higher than Sieg- Idealists in famous novels fried's. The romantic temper incapable of seeing the world except through its own veil of rosy gauze, lost in its introspective dreams and vagaries, has been pilloried forever by Cervantes, and yet in that vein of Spanish high comedy which leaves Don Quixote the world's loved fool. Bespattered with unsavory mud, he can be pathetic at moments, but never tragic. On his feet again, he looks out on the monotonous plain of La Mancha, and sees towers with lovely captives, knights in glorified armor, courts and palaces the Arab might envy. After all, his delusions are essentially harmless. He is not really caught in the shock of life-experience at all. Moreover, one important point must be grasped. His idealism consists in glorifying the *past*. Humanity is ever ready to indulge this glow of reminiscence in which we all share. It is when the idealist tries to indulge his dreams of a future which *he alone sees*, that the novelist rightly pictures him coming to grief, or to ineffectual tragedy.

Such an idealist we find in Turgenev's marvellous portrait of Rudin, in the novel of the same name. Here is a man with the fiery eloquence of the early Russian liberal, full of ideals which he cannot realize and yet will not compromise. He understands the path of compromise clearly enough. There would be no actual difficulty for him so far as ability goes.

The inevitable crises always find him half-way towards realization. If he could persuade himself that yielding something of his principle might bring him nearer to his goal, he could make the ordinary drive for success. But he never sees anything as possible except blank refusal. He becomes a failing wanderer. He has never been able to carry out his ideals; nor yet has he attained comfort, success, happiness. His old school-fellow, Lezhnyoff, who has all these things, sitting by his warm fire with the driving storm outside, persuades Dmitri Rudin to spend a cozy evening with him. They talk as Russians often will about their intimate aims and losses. It is the fortunate man who salutes the failure. To fail on such terms has greatness in it. There is no easy refuge for Rudin, even in his friend's kindness. The crackle of the fire, the safety of the little human circle are not for him. The contrast is vividly dramatized for the reader when the door closes on the lonely, aging man who must go back into the storm and the dark night. Just then a wild gust of wind rattles the panes, and we are left to imagine the wanderer without.

We do not see him again until the last gesture of his death in the workingmen's revolt of 1848 in Paris. Here they do not even know his nationality, but call him "The Pole", as he is picked off the barricade, a tall, gaunt figure with gray, dishevelled hair, a shabby old coat with red scarf, and a dull sword. He rushes up the barricade waving his red flag, and offers himself, a splendid, useless target for the sharpshooters. He has not even realized that the fighting is over and the cause lost. Well for him, perhaps, since he can die in the glow of his ideal. How clearly his problem stands forth for the discerning reader! Rudin and his like act only from within, achieving a kind of magnificent self-expression. They do not measure results. They do not even take serious pains to make their aims intelligible, or progressively intelligible. They never ask themselves "What could I have done to make my ideas clearer in my last mishap?" They cannot direct their undoubted powers to any foreseen end. The tragedy is thus the greater, the pathos of Rudin's life the more poignant.

The idealist in fiction usually has personal courage. Don Quixote charges up to his windmills with a fine gesture. In *Lord Jim*, however, Conrad has given us the idealist united with the coward. Jim's romantic dreams of heroic splendor, as he paced athwart the bridge of his ship and looked out on to the peaceful sea, had never been tested by actual crisis. It was always in the calm, safe rhythm of the ship's motion on favorable nights that he had the finest visions of himself as a hero. On such a night the test came, and found him unequal to the ordinary seaman's plain duty. He spent the rest of his life recovering his belief in himself. He won it in one last courageous, proud moment of facing death, but again it is idealism with no reference to practical results. He acted entirely from within, his eye on his ideal of himself, without a thought of benefit or loss to others.

This does not mean, of course, that the idealist invariably acts in this way, even in fiction. Still less could we draw any fixed conclusions about the idealist in life itself. It is merely worth remarking that the distinguished portraits in novels often have this trait. Even when the idealist is voicing the author's own favorite beliefs, like Dostoiefsky's Ivan Shatov in *The Possessed*, he can only get himself murdered without adding strength to the cause. Not a single soul believes in mystical Russia more fervently because of Shatov. He has talked about his faith in Holy Russia at length, and explained his ideal for her to save the world. But he cannot even make his position straight in his social world. He does not know how to disentangle himself from a band of revolutionaries with whom he is totally out of sympathy. It would be quite unfair, however, not to recognize that these idealists are aglow with

189

all that has most dignified human life. Furthermore, we must always beware of our American tendency to examine results too sharply according to
fixed standards. The results of a heroic ideal may
be obscure and intangible as yet, but their force is
certain to be felt in the future.

Closely related to the idealist and more or less
identified with him is the ascetic. Savonarola, as
George Eliot drew him in *Romola*, will
occur to every reader as typical. He represents only the active reformer among them,
however, and we observe the concentrated drive
which his intense devotion to one single cause gives
him. He immolates himself; but he also immolates
everyone who will let him do so, and everything
about him that he can lay his hands on. It is all one
grand bonfire to God. The contemplative ascetic
lives more quietly in his mystic devotion. His
austerities are usually more purely personal. Fogazzaro has given an admirable portrait of the religious devotee in his novel, *The Saint*, in which
Piero Maironi, although outside the regular orders
of the church, lives the life of the stern ascetic combined with that of the reformer. The pure mystic
type, however, with its absorption in contemplation,
is clearly described by George Moore in *The Lake*.
Father Oliver, the Irish priest, has a poetic quality

The ascetic in fiction

190

in his Celtic mysticism. His gentle, lonely contemplations near the lake appeal to every reader's sympathy. It is the more surprising, therefore, to find that a vein of cruelty runs through his life, as well as through the others whom we have mentioned.

Here is a fine opportunity for close analysis. The cruelty shows itself especially towards the woman they might have loved, or do love in spite of their refusal to admit it. Obviously the roots of it lie very deep, and are very difficult to reach. Probably he is taking some obscure revenge for his unnatural life, by punishing the very being who reminds him of it. Or he may be taking some unconscious satisfaction by way of the cruelty itself. However we explain it, the fact is significantly present in almost every notable ascetic in fiction, unless we except the simple village priest, *Le Curé de Village*, as portrayed by Balzac and others. The good shepherd of the village flock has so many normal human interests in the lives which he knows so intimately, in the affairs of his parish which keep him so wholesomely busy, that he preserves a sane, sweet temper.

Perhaps the most varied and dramatic contrasts in character are to be found in the great portrait gallery of "fallen sisters" in fiction. We cannot trace any single predominating trait here. There is that merciless little "Fallen Sisters" in fiction adventuress Becky Sharp, in her mid-Victorian frame. Not a word to be said for her by her creator except that she is clever! There is Emma Bovary, eating her heart out in provincial boredom until she reaches greedily for any new sensation. There are the baleful, destructive sirens of Turgenev, restless and dominating, never contented with their prey. There beside them belongs Hardy's Eustacia Vye, desperate for escape from her hated Egdon Heath. But Hardy calls his Tess a pure woman, and lavishes upon her his admiring sympathy. Dostoiefsky's Sonia, in *Crime and Punishment*, sells herself to bring food to her stepmother and her children. Dostoiefsky regards her as little short of the angels. She carries the Testament with her, does errands for the prisoners, redeems the murderer, and is very generally beloved. She ends, too, in the orthodox Christian life. Her "yellow ticket" was but a passing incident. It did not scorch the pure soul. George Moore's Esther Waters is regarded by those who were most familiar with her history as the best woman they had ever known. Sheila Kaye Smith's Joanna Godden is cast in a heroic mould. Like a woman of some old saga, she can face the loss of her moors, and go forth to disgrace if need be with a vivid sense of the fullness of living. Perhaps the most thoroughly human of them all is Julia Peterkin's *Scarlet Sister Mary*, who is neither idealized nor sentimentalized, but stands there before us in all her grossness, — warm-blooded, large-hearted, humorous, clever, courageous, superstitious, and intensely vain. Certainly it may be said that novelists in general have not regarded "fallen sisters" according to conventional codes.

We could continue the list of types almost indefinitely. Teachers particularly could glance with profit at the sorry figure cut by the school-master in fiction. At least it is worth while to ask ourselves why he has been a butt for ridicule. A burlesque villain like Squeers, or a wheezing, psalm-singing pedant like Ichabod Crane fleeing in terror from the first practical joke not set down in his books for him to learn. An intellectual fool, usually. One or two fine headmasters hardly alter the general impression. Is it owing to the servant tradition of teaching? The teacher has often been a sort of upper servant. Or is it owing rather to a habit of taking life at second or even third hand?

The schoolmaster in fiction

We come now more definitely to the question of approach in detail. How shall we proceed in reading the great character novels? How should our techniques differ from those of the approach to masterpieces of pure art? We saw that we should

193

regard the work of art as a whole, for a complete æsthetic experience of quiet appreciation, usually slower than one's ordinary tempo. In ap-

Techniques for reading character novels

proaching the character-novels, it will easily be observed, even in the slight analyses here, that every minor matter seems to drop away before these compelling por-

traits. They hold the centre of attention so completely, that to give equal regard to other details would be almost like paying as much heed to the frames or the wainscoting in a picture gallery, as one pays to the portraits. The settings are to be noted in passing as appropriate or not. And that is about all. In the discussion of these great character-novels with a thousand college students in the past ten years, it has been significant that whatever the subject of the moment, the questions of character become almost perforce uppermost at once. The challenge is immediate, human, not to be disregarded. The teacher of literature who turns Don Quixote into a study of La Mancha in the early seventeenth century is thwarting not only Cervantes but the mental growth of the students. Even advanced classes need the character emphasis first of all. The novel is the greatest vehicle for conveying character to human readers. Should not our techniques be evolved from this central fact? One would suppose, from some procedures, that the central aim in reading Dickens, for instance, is to make our students into writers on *The London that Charles Dickens Knew*, or *The Inns that Charles Dickens visited*, or *Tally-Ho with Dickens*. Such pamphlets may be useful, but they represent very highly specialized objectives. The general flavor of such inns as The Bull in Rochester will be quite sufficient for the reader of Dickens, who is always at his best in his gallery of human characters. Therefore, in general we should read with deliberate focus on the characters, taking our fairly rapid rates of reading for all the rest of the novel.

In this careful attention to the characters, we should slow down very considerably where they are sketched at length, or highly dramatized before us. Sometimes we shall want to mark critical scenes for cross comparison with others, not to the extent of actual re-reading, perhaps, although this may well be involved when it is a matter of following the subtle changes in development. If we follow Tito Melema in George Eliot's *Romola*, we shall soon note the well-marked stages in his degeneration. Silas Lapham, too, and Bartley Hubbard show notable differences as their stories proceed. It will be well to mark the important passages, or at least keep them well in mind. All this means pausing now and then to note definitely the progress of character, or the crises of character. The reading is not one steady act of appreciation, but is properly disjointed with pauses and questions. We stop to be sure we seized a certain point, to think about it, to surround it with questions. The condition of reflection here often lies in the hero's problem. Would he have solved it in this way? Is it really natural? Probable? Genuine, sound psychology, or theatrical, for effect chiefly? The purely human values should be first in our thinking, and yet it is obvious that very close and valuable interlocking with problems of psychology and sociology could be effected with the situations in novels as a basis. Questions should be deliberate, constant, varied, and penetrating.

What is the effect, for instance, of prolonged monotony in landscape, toil, amusement, or relationship? What happens to the personality of one who forces himself to make social contacts which he inwardly despises? What will the race for success do to the reflective temperament? What are the most subtle modes of domination? Of escape? Of failure? What is the effect of enforced contact upon opposing wills? Such questions abound in both the older and new fiction.

If novels can sometimes be compared to a portrait gallery, they can also in many instances be com-

pared to a gallery of landscapes. These are spe-
cifically the novels in which the influence of Nature
is dominant. Nature indeed becomes the
chief actor in the drama, even though the **We reflect on the influence of Nature in novels**
drama is one of human life. The charac-
ters are like the more or less unimportant
figures in a Dutch landscape of Ruisdael
or Hobbema. The comparison underestimates the
human values in any novel, but it will serve to
clarify a general distinction which is entirely valid.
The landscape against which the little human lives
are played out is there long before they come, de-
termines their little moment, and will be there long
after they have gone. They are caught in elemental
forces. The struggle is sometimes superb, and seems
for a moment to make "giants in the earth" of rather
petty beings, who win their fields from the hands of
Nature after years of toil. Nevertheless, we are
never allowed to forget that Nature towers above
them. The rhythm of her seasons is their litany.
Her suns and her frosts are their gods and their
devils, demanding the obedience of slaves. **Knut**
The great novel of this class is Knut **Hamsun's Growth of the Soil**
Hamsun's *Growth of the Soil*. Isak, the
rough Nordland hero of the wild Norwegian highlands, knows nothing but the laws of
the relentless seasons. He is ugly to look at, bent

from his heavy work in the fields, a mere "barge of a man" outlined against the northern sky with the rhythmic swirl of his arm as he sows his grain. He has no calendar, and does not even know the days of the month, except St. Olaf's in the autumn, when the hay must be in. The other characters are elemental also. They fail when they go to the cities and try to learn "sales patter." They must come back to the fields which claim them, and to which they belong. Hardships and elemental cruelties make no difference. Ordinary human tragedies are little episodes between the planting and the harvest, or between the harvest and the slow springtime. The only important events are the snows covering the rough cart-tracks through the dark winter, the warm furrows of earth under the light spring sky, the towering highlands in the midnight sun, and the bare, harvested fields on St. Olaf's Day, with the first snows in the air again. These facts are the inescapable realities that determine all else. Human life itself is a brief unnoticed span in comparison. Yet there is a strange, epic quality in the march of the seasons. Two recent French novels present dominant Nature in a similar way. One is Chateaubriand's *Peatcutters* and the other is André Chamson's *The Road*, which has been called a French *Growth of the Soil*. Björnson's *Arne, the Fisher Maiden* also makes us experience the keen, pine-scented northern air as the real essence of his story.

Even with Leatherstocking and Long Tom Coffin in the balance, the real protagonist of Cooper's best novels is Nature. The virgin forest mirrored in deep inland lakes, the danger trail over high precipices, the quivering early green of birches, the dew on the oak in the morning, the sunset through lordly pines in the evening, — these, and such as these, are Cooper's chief characters. French critics like Balzac have called him a superlative landscape artist. What is Leatherstocking himself but an expression of life in the primitive forests? No wonder this trail-hunter, this pathfinder, this hawkeye, this deer-slayer, called Nature his sweetheart. She is that, but also more than that. She is the great Mother of his life as well, forming it from his earliest years. She is dominant.

Nature dominant in James Fenimore Cooper

The primitive tropical forests and the vast reaches of South American pampas also form the chief interests of the fascinating English writer, W. H. Hudson. His forest life takes on a mystical quality in *Green Mansions*, embodied in the strange bird-maiden, Rima. The expanse of the prairie, the quiver of light in the dense, tall, tropical trees are paramount, even though savage customs, minor movements of

Nature dominant in W. H. Hudson's novels

199

early settlers, a few human characters of some importance emerge now and then. Wild, tropical, or semi-tropical Nature is his great protagonist.

Discriminating readers will make a fine distinction just here. The novels of Hamsun, Cooper, Hudson, and many others of the same general type, devoted to dominant Nature, will not be confused with great human stories like those of Thomas Hardy, in which Nature is an important "environing action", determining in part the cast of character and destiny, but at most forming the background of living experience, never taking the central place of the actual driving force, even in *The Return of the Native*, where Egdon Heath approaches this importance. Human tragedy set off against elemental forces may be studied to better advantage in a remarkable group of sociological novels reserved for the next chapter.

Distinction between Nature dominant and Nature as a background

If the landscapes or the natural, elemental forces of Nature are the most important aspects of any novel, how shall we adapt our reading to fit them? Is not the best technique partially indicated in the facts? We shall concentrate on the very aspects which we ignore in the novel of character. We shall take the characters more or

Techniques for reading the novel of landscape or elemental Nature

200

less for granted. Even Leatherstocking, fine, manly scout of the woods, is very simple. His fairness, kindness, tolerance of the "red man's gifts", quiet worship of Nature, unequalled marksmanship, keen scent on the trail, loyalty to his friends, — all these traits are plain from the first, with no problems. And Leatherstocking is more highly individualized than many other figures in this type of story. Usually we can pass with fair rapidity over the narrative itself, and pause, or at least slow down markedly, for the landscapes, or seascapes, or their influence on the human beings concerned. The condition of reflection here is not so much in problems as in the realization of the power, or the vastness, or the indifference, or the cruelty, or the beauty of Nature. Such realization takes time. It means a slower rate for the descriptive passages, and a deliberate attention upon them, rather than pausing to ask questions as in the case of the character novel. Sometimes cross references to various parts of the novel will be useful. To mark the passages showing the effect of the seasons in the Nordland, for instance, in reading *Growth of the Soil*, might intensify one's sense of the natural, inevitable sharp contrasts in the far north. Usually, however, all this will be clear in slowed-down rates of reading. Another aid more valuable still is the attempt to visualize the scenes by deliberately calling to mind all the similar scenes one has known. Students from different parts of the world can contribute a great deal to one another in this regard.

We have discussed the quiet æsthetic experience of reading the novels which are masterpieces of art, and found that they need a rather consistently slow rate of reading for the appreciation to sink in, yet without pauses of any length. The object should be before us in its entirety. On the other hand, problems of personality in the character novel will require many pauses for questions, with cross references and comparisons of states of mind, noting always the progress or growth or degeneration. Finally we have seen that the novel showing the dominant influence of Nature should be read with emphasis on the descriptive scenes. All these modes require a rate considerably slower than one's fastest reading rates, but differing, of course, with individual judgment. Our best students vary their rates most freely, as our tests have shown. Should the rate for any entire novel be slowed down to reading aloud? Bear in mind that this means forcing the rapidly travelling eye down to the rate implied in oral vocalization.

Shall we read novels aloud?

If we apply vocalization to novel-reading, we are forcing a much slower pace than is natural for novel-reading, by and large. Broadly speaking, fiction belongs to the material for rapid, silent reading. Even the great character novels have scenes of less importance which can be skimmed or skipped entirely. Reading a book through aloud does not allow for any changes in rate, and proceeds at much too slow a rate as a rule. For reading aloud it is much better to choose material demand-ing a thinking pace more suited to the slow voice, such as essays, poetry, history, drama, or science. **Two reasons for not reading novels aloud, as a rule**

Secondly, novels do not usually need to be heard in order to be appreciated. They are not among the auditory experiences by nature. If we think of the long history of poetry allied with its twin sister music, of the drama allied with both, and all three meant to be heard from the beginning, and from their very nature, we shall have a criterion at once for the read-ing of fiction aloud.

What parts of a novel shall we actually share by reading aloud? Obviously, those very scenes which suggest drama or poetry. There are pas-sages in Dickens which could be rendered on the stage with scarcely the change of a word. They fairly shout their demand to be heard. Indeed the best introduc-tion to a complicated Dickens novel is often the dramatic presentation of memorable "acting" parts, **Read aloud only poetic and dramatic scenes**

— the Podsnaps giving an evening ball, the Wilfers receiving Mrs. Boffin, the scenes in Boffin's Bower, Mr. Pecksniff on the inside of the coach, Oliver Twist asking for more, and many others that will occur to the reader at once. These have been spoken scenes ever since Dickens himself read them aloud. More rarely a passage from Thackeray makes the same demand. "The campaigner" shouting at "Mr. Pendennis" in *The Newcomes* is one example. Not to have heard this chapter read aloud would be a sure loss. Yet to read the whole of *The Newcomes* aloud would be an even surer loss of time and emphasis. Similarly Meredith's *Egoist* is not a novel to be read aloud as a whole. Yet Sir Willoughby Patterne's final proposal to Laetitia is a little one-scene play which should certainly be heard. We often have these scenes when the novel rises to its climax. Less often does the novel approach poetry. There are, however, descriptive passages of such rare beauty that they may well be shared through sympathetic reading aloud. Instances will occur to every reader. It is a matter of personal choice, very largely, but we might advise in passing that the impressive descriptions of Hardy's Egdon Heath, the frozen lakes of Selma Lagerlöf, the village scenes of Balzac, and the Russian country life of Turgenev should be shared with the most appreciative readers we know.

CHAPTER VII

WHEN SHALL WE STUDY THE NOVEL?

The reflective enjoyment of masterpieces of art does not imply study, in the strict sense. The appreciative pause should not be interrupted with problems. Even the questions of character and of the influence of Nature in fiction are so immediate in their universal appeal that they hardly constitute any such assembling of facts, causes, results, or ideas as we need in definite study. Here and there, it is true, we refer to some previous passage in reflecting on our hero's problem, as we have seen in our last chapter. We may wish to mark pages for comparison. But the whole content is so easily known through our sympathetic emotions as we read, that the term study would, in general, be a misnomer.

Distinction between reflection and study

Study implies a central problem of tougher fibre, a matter of some difficulty in relating the facts for its solution. It implies organizing data to find that solution. It implies further sifting of the data to select only the most relevant for the issue. It implies finally some synthesis or conclusion, or at least some marked trend indicated by the facts after prolonged analysis. Obviously the poised enjoyment of beauty for its own sake is as unlike formal study as the contemplation of Leonardo's Last Supper in Milan is unlike a lawyer's summary in the court of appeals.

To what extent shall we apply the techniques of actual study to novels? Would it be misapplied

To what extent should we apply actual study to novels? energy in any case? The answer seems to be indicated in the conditions. If we have genuine problems of this sort in novel-reading, it will be worth while to study them. But it will be decidedly a waste of time to manufacture such problems for factitious reasons as teachers of English have sometimes done. What sorts of topics or questions demand actual study in any novel? The problems must naturally be outside the immediate range of the student's knowledge and sympathy. The struggles of personality alone are too near to any ordinary reader, too easy to apprehend at once, for actual study. True, they may be related in many ways to psychological material, and may even furnish excellent illustrations for psychological studies. On the whole, they are very easy, very human, very compelling, except in the new novels of the subconscious. This new cult does often need study for actual comprehension. We have also two other types of novels which may profitably be studied. They are social and satirical novels. We will consider these three classes in order.

The cult of the subconscious has its precursors in the dramatic monologues of Browning, and in the long soliloquies of the older spoken drama. A series of impressions purely subjective in treatment, while not essentially new in form, has yet been rendered new and difficult in fiction by the attempt to seize the stream of feeling below the surface of the **I. The cult of the subconscious in the new fiction** conscious life. The depth of subjectivity thus achieved makes Browning's *Last Duchess* seem an affair of the footlights. Impressions become incoherent in the fiction of the subconscious, because they express the play of instinct, of impulses, before they are organized even for the conscious mind to take note of, still less for public presentation. The raw stuff of experience is dressed for its part in the wings before it comes onto the stage of life, in the view of these writers who prefer to catch the elusive impulse in its first form, if they can. Hence we have the result in conflicting half-statements, syncopated phrases, truncated ideas through which the bewildered reader has to guess his way.

A few of the suggestions which have helped our students may be in order. First of all we must never forget that we are not in any actual scene in these novels. We are in the consciousness of the character chosen by the author. We see nothing objectively, therefore, but on the contrary we must learn to wander in a maze of impressions on the inside of the life. We are to become aware of what the character himself is hardly aware. If we recall for ourselves some crisis of our own past, we shall see little details cropping out which we did not know we were observing at all, at the time. While we were consciously agonizing over some acute problem, apparently to the exclusion of everything else, we were noting subconsciously the children building a snow-man, the sun flashing on the silver tea-urn, etc., etc. All this put together in its entirety would be incoherent. Yet we shall have a remarkable sense of the life-process itself if we try to follow what at first seems unintelligent chaos.

Suggestions for reading the novel of the subconscious

This is not the whole difficulty, alas! Having altered our stand as readers from the objective to the subjective we are called upon to shift without notice from present to past, from past to future, from dream to reminiscence, from wish to reality. We cannot be sure in any given instance whether our hero is dreaming of himself as he might have been, or may be, or has been; whether he is recalling what his mother thought him to be; whether he is dramatizing to himself some vision of other characters; or whether he is simply noting what is. In such difficulties, what should the reader do? Certainly he should not linger too long over any passage, but holding all these possibilities in mind, travel on. The main thing of importance is to keep the subjective point of view. The trend of personality will gradually become clear. Fortunately for the unpractised reader this new fiction repeats a good deal, and what is not clear at once will become reasonably clear with repetition.

We say "reasonably clear" advisedly. If the reader finds himself too bewildered, let him take assurance from the differences among notable critics. They are often in disagreement as to the interpretation of James Joyce, D. H. Lawrence, Mrs. Woolf, Dorothy Richardson, and others. Furthermore, the reader will gradually learn to interpret for himself as he would learn a new language. Indeed the expression of the incoherent animal flow of life is like a new language, which gradually disengages itself from the objective facts as we usually know them.

Another suggestion which may be useful in reading these difficult novels is to throw overboard any notion of plot, story, or even events in the ordinary sense. Seven or eight chapters may not take us any further than the heroine's thoughts between Trafalgar Square and Westminster. We must carefully delete all the standards for a coherent, planned, purposeful story that we have ever learned. They do not apply. We must rather look for a revelation of the depth of raw impulse below the polished surfaces of life. If we accustom ourselves to look for it, we shall succeed in changing our point of view. In other words, we must develop new criteria for the cult of the subconscious in fiction.

It is in many respects as difficult as learning a new language. Possibly some readers will consider it considerably less rewarding. The remarkable sense of seeing actual emotional roots of experience, however, will compensate most readers for the effort. It should be remembered, also, that coherent, ordered thought, matured planning, deliberate art can never permanently go out of style. We shall wake up some day to find that they stand for considerable human achievement. After the welter of chaotic impulses we shall regard connected thought as refreshing again, although the study of the elemental drive of emotion has been extremely valuable in fiction.

Another group of novels should be studied in a different way. They are the social novels actually contributing to the understanding of certain environments.   They are not character-novels, primarily, nor yet landscape novels of local color, but they combine the two types into a synthesis of **II. Novels** human life in some definite chosen region **as social** intimately known to the writer.   Here we **studies** are well out beyond the bounds of mere **definite** story.   The dominant interest is always **social** in large social groups, or typical members **influences** of such groups, in their modes of thought, codes of action, customs and manners, not merely as they afford a chance for the picturesque, but because of their relentless conditioning of human experience. A brief comparison will make this class of novel stand out plainly before us.

If we recall once more the most famous novels of character, such as *Tom Jones*, *Don Quixote*, *Tristram Shandy*, *David Copperfield*, *Vanity Fair*, and others, we shall picture at once the personal figures in them, towering above every detail of their surroundings. We could piece out a study of Becky Sharp's London that would not be without interest, but would her adventures be essentially different in any large capital?   Differences in character there would certainly be in another environment.   We do not picture Becky as merely the expression of a human environment.   She is herself, individual, unique, and the details of place and time are irrelevant in

211

comparison to her personality. Now if we shift the scene to the novels of Galsworthy and Arnold Bennett, what do we find? An emphasis on the social situation so great that even their most vivid characters are subordinate to it.

A little exercise or game will bring this fact out admirably. After our students have been reading both classes of novels for some months, it is amusing for them to put down off-hand as many names of characters in novels as they can, in an impromptu memory contest. The names of David Copperfield, Micawber, Uriah Heep, Becky Sharp, Pendennis, Clarissa Harlowe, Tom Jones, Maggie Tulliver, Bella Wilfer, the Boffins, Sary Gamp, and many others from the character novels will stand out in almost any student's impromptu list, while many a good reader has been unable to remember the exact names of Arnold Bennett's characters. The very titles of many modern novels show the extraordinary shift of interest to social problems. *The Man of Property*, *The Country House*, *Fraternity*, *The Five Towns*, all suggest types or large social groupings. Soames Forsyte, for instance, is not a person for and by himself as Becky Sharp is. Soames represents the upper middle class of England in its economic and social life. He is, in fact, very exactly the man of property.

212

Many other examples will occur at once to the reader. Hamlin Garland's *Son of the Middle Border*, *Daughter of the Middle Border*, *Trail-* Other *Makers of the Middle Border* convey their notable themes in their titles. *Main Street* has examples become a national symbol. Willa Cather's of socio-logical immigrant pioneers of Nebraska have be- trends in come regional types of national impor- fiction tance. Whoever wants to know what Salem was in the heyday of its clipper ships will not neglect Hergesheimer's *Java Head*.

But for the precursor of all these novelists we must go to Balzac with his *Comédie humaine* in many volumes. Balzac deliberately planned a Balzac as long series of interlocking novels to express precursor the human comedy itself with a scope in the hitherto unknown. Vast scenes in the *Comédie humaine* country life of central France, as well as in Paris, were directed towards the interplay of human lives with their conditioning surroundings, their houses, their shops, their agriculture, their commerce, their architecture, their rural and city systems of ethics, religions, and philosophy. "Comedy" is to be understood here only in its intellectual sense of the incongruity in human life, over which gods might laugh, perhaps, but which is not necessarily funny to human eyes. On the contrary, the scene may often have a marked sadness, like the unconscious pathos of the good country doctor in his neat, trellised garden, telling his long story with the volubility of a lonely man to the first stranger, in *Le Médecin de Campagne*. This is only one of the *Scènes de la Vie de Campagne*, designed to present country life in all its aspects, with all its characteristic problems. The individual is always sunk in the group-interest. *Le Curé de Village*, for instance, is just the village priest in his ideal form, absorbed in his village problems. In like manner *César Birotteau* shows the city shopkeeper rising out of his class, a French version of *The Rise of Silas Lapham*. In all these cases, however, it is the conditioning society which forms the actual theme.

No such deliberate emphasis on social groups is to be found in Russian fiction. Yet there is a surprising amount of incidental revelation of the **Social motif in Russian fiction** general life beyond the bounds of the story proper. Even an impersonal artist like Turgenev catches the meaning of embryonic revolutionary movements so exactly that the very word "nihilist" comes from his novel *Fathers and Sons*, and was first used there to describe the spirit of denial in the younger generation. Within a short time the word was in common use to denote a social reality. *Virgin Soil* carried the movement one step further. His *Sportsman's Sketches* present the sad, sordid, and absurd details in the lives of the oppressed peasants so vividly that the emancipation of the serfs owes no small debt to them. From an entirely different point of view Dostoiefsky's pictures of revolutionary groups in *The Possessed* and in *Crime and Punishment* should be studied by any reader who wishes to understand Russia.

In fact it is quite possible to reconstruct a fairly complete picture of ante-bellum Russia from her writers of fiction. Those country houses, for example, are as clear in their pages as if we could observe the originals to-day. The owners were of course people of wealth, either of the nobility or of high official standing under the Czar. They took their retinue of servants down to their country seats from St. Petersburg, along with their books, their musical instruments, their pictures, and their clothes. But they fondly believed that their manners came from Paris. They welcomed any visitor who could talk of the great capital of cosmopolitan culture. They played up to him in their best French, which was generally better than their Russian, since they prided themselves on forgetting the language of the serfs. They were self-exiled in their own land, always longing for the next transcontinental express to Paris, or Baden, or possibly Venice and Rome.

The height of their social ambition at home was reached when they could hear their guests discussing the Paris season after dinner on the terrace, and could feel with an absurd provincial thrill, "How like a French salon!"

The other side of the picture is no less clear. Where could any student gain so true an idea of the contrasts between north and south in Russia, as by reading Turgenev's *Sportsman's Sketches* of life among the peasants in central and northern Russia, and Gogol's *Evenings on a Farm near Dikanka?* Gogol writes of the joyous peasants in the suave climate of the Ukraine as they gather for stories at the neat cottage of Rudy Panko, the bee-keeper. Turnovers and cream, dumplings with mulled vodka are always on the way. The cottages are often painted in gay colors, with fierce Cossack riders outlined on the doors. The village fairs are aflame with a riot of beads, chains, embroidery, horse-trappings, and the like. On Christmas morning before daybreak the village church is filled with women in white linen wimples, or green blouses with gold streamers behind. Amid the bright confusion of ribbons, crosses, necklaces, and beads, they all press towards the ikon-stand.

How different the thatched grey huts of Turgenev's serfs in Great Russia! The reader never

216

forgets their sordid serfdom, their poverty, their few pleasures in the summer, their long, slothful sleep on the stove through the winter snows. Now and then one of them sings rather well to the balalaika, and enjoys the grouse hunting or the bee-keeping, the splash of the ducks, or the flight of the cranes above. But, on the whole, all is sordid or tragic.

Often the novel of social life uses Nature or the local environment for effects in contrast, throwing the central theme into strong light or shadow. Elizabeth Roberts's fine novel, *The Time of Man*, thus plays the constant shifting of the restless poor whites against the quiet night sky of the South. We begin with the wagon rattling over the hills under the stars; and we end with the same impression of wide, aimless wandering emphasized by the unchanging night. Does it not make the civilized reader feel a little house-bound?

Use of Nature as contrast in social novels

Such a use of Nature does not make her the chief protagonist of the action, by any means, but it does increase the subtleties of the human drama. In Hardy's novels we have a constant sense of the sombre landscape of southwest England; yet the characters, after all, are highly individualized, no matter how strongly the heath has influenced them. Willa Cather's *Death Comes for the Archbishop* heightens the hardships of her missionaries by the use of the desert and the mesa. Stark Young's *Heaven Trees* gets the very meaning of the plantation garden of the far South into his action. Louis Bromfield's *Green Bay Tree* shows an admirable use of contrast in describing the garden on Cypress Hill, with its high hedge scorched by gases from the manufacturing centre slowly surrounding it and eclipsing its formal, reminiscent splendor, its Apollo Belvedere, its dust-powdered flowers. In such details we can see the actual conflict of two different eras dramatized before us. Often the novelist can relieve the effect of too great human suffering, as in Turgenev's *Yermolai and the Miller's Wife*, by setting it against the cool, refreshing mist from the river, the drip of the mill-wheels in the keen air, the whizzing of the wild ducks, and the nightingale's song. Thus Nature's perpetual renewals are subtly indicated. We are quietly made to feel the shortness of human agony beside the long-flowing river.

The analysis of these few examples of the social novel reveals the natural emphasis of importance for the reader. While the novel of personality, as we have seen, carries one swiftly into a central life situation of compelling interest, the novel primarily of social value has its rich treasures em-

Techniques for reading the novel of social values

218

bedded in apparently trivial details which would be easy to miss. Therefore we have found it most helpful to our students to recommend two readings, the first a rapid survey of the story for its broad human interests, and the second a carefully planned re-reading for the details of life in the region of the novel, and a resulting summary of them. What is it like to be a furze-cutter, a sheep farmer, a shoemaker, a van driver, a vicar of the village church in Hardy's Wessex? How do the peasant tenants actually live? Why is the heath unproductive? What makes grim thought-patterns natural in the district? What do the yeoman farmers talk about at the bars of the village inn? Consider the richness of detail in this seemingly unimportant paragraph from *The Return of the Native:*

> On Egdon there was no absolute hour of the day. The time at any moment was a number of varying doctrines professed by the different hamlets . . . West Egdon believed in Blooms-end time, East Egdon in the time of the Quiet Woman Inn. Grandfer Cantle's watch had numbered many followers in years gone by, but since he had grown older, faiths were shaken . . .

Definite re-reading, then, should reconstruct the life of the region. But re-reading alone is not enough, even if accompanied by marking characteristic bits now and then. Rather should the significant details be gathered together in the student's note-book for ready reference. Afterwards they will form the basis for a useful little written review, perhaps covering the material of several novels. The vivid sense of life, including the typical industries, habits, general outlook, points of view, range of culture, and so on, will be a genuine reward to the student for his pains. He will have a richer understanding of all shopkeepers of the lower middle class in England, for example, when he has realized in this way the sitting-room over the shop in Arnold Bennett's novels of the potteries, — that sitting-room which becomes a dining room with the clatter of heavy trays at high tea.

Here for the first time in our reading of novels we come upon the desirability of using reference books, industrial and social histories of a region, maps, guides, illustrated travel volumes, portraits, landscapes, drawings, and talks with travellers. These can be illuminating if always used long after the first appreciative reading of a book. They should mark a late stage in the approach, never a stampede of the young reader before the book has been enjoyed for its own sake. For that first reading the fewer minimal essentials of preliminary guidance, the better. The testimony of college students whose natural approach to classical novels has been ruined by maps and charts is explicit. We have heard it from hundreds. Only the picturesque general details of a region like Hardy's Wessex should accompany the first reading. Afterwards the student who has learned to appreciate Hardy's austere beauty will relish a detailed study of hamlets like Little Hintock and Bockhampton, will trace lovingly Hardy's own evolution from the thatched farmhouse where he was born, and will notice with keen interest that in just such fine old houses lived Gabriel Oak and William Dewy.

Overlapping other types of fiction in some respects, yet for reading purposes forming a class by itself, is the satirical novel. Even the broad strokes **Satirical** of Mark Twain in *Captain Stormfield's Visit* **novels** *to Heaven* deserves much thought. When the good Captain who has entered Heaven almost unobserved sees the host of archangels turning out in a vast parade to welcome a notorious repentant sinner, he ruefully admits that his angel guide is right in warning him that it is too late to make up lost opportunities on earth. He cannot go back and become a picturesque sinner. Just as staggering to his composure is the knowledge that they have never heard of America in Heaven, and that it can only be located after prolonged search on the outskirts of the universe in the solar system of Jupiter. Worst of all the whole earth itself is known in Heaven as the Wart. The conceit of the human race is more subtly indicated in *The Mysterious Stranger*, but it involves the same ironic overturn in our ordinary perspective.

Much more difficult is Meredith's satire. Not only the allusive, involved style, but the depth of rich surprise in his thought makes a serious enterprise for the reader. Robert Louis Stevenson, a swift, voracious, and talented reader, felt, after re-reading *The Egoist* for the fourth time, that it would take six or seven re-readings to comprehend it thoroughly. Sir Willoughby Patterne is not just a portrait. He is a system, a code, a travesty, and an innuendo. The wit of Anatole France, also, has many involved references. Even behind his lightest Gallic jest which may seem stark indecency to Anglo-Saxon readers there will lurk an ironic commentary on life which it would be a pity to miss. The same is true of the mordant satire of Aldous Huxley.

In the hands of writers like Dean Swift and Samuel Butler satire can become positively savage. A more recent example is Luigi Pirandello's *Si Gira*, a terrific commentary on the machine age. Here we have the film operator, Serafino Gubbio, turning the handle of his machine for the grand tiger finale. One of the actors is to shoot the tiger for a film sensation. Instead, the tiger crushes the actor, and the sensation becomes unintentionally greater because Gubbio, although filled with horror, is so well trained that he mechanically keeps on turning the handle. The machine is thus shown to be all-powerful in the face of human agony.

A charming group of delicate and fanciful satires afford equally penetrating glimpses of life, and equally caustic criticisms of it, although written in such a different mood and tempo. Elinor Wylie, Sylvia Warner, and Margaret Kennedy have used a rare art in their lightest pages. This is particularly true of Sylvia Warner's *Lolly Willowes*, that delightful rebellious spirit of Puck in the Victorian spinster who refuses to be called Aunt an hour longer, and flees gleefully to the mist and rain of the English countryside. The quaint, fanciful, eerie mirth only throws into clearer relief the heavy Victorian drawing-room where Aunt Lolly had played her absurd part of the dependent regarded as a child.

Elinor Wylie's *Venetian Glass Nephew*, *The Orphan Angel*, and *Mr. Hodge and Mr. Hazard* are mere fantasies, in one sense, and yet the delicate satire wrapped up in their dainty folds deserves study. Was the romanticist temper ever more piquantly indicated than in Mr. Hazard? Not only the cape

223

and broad hat, the pallor and the magnificent gestures, but the haughty reticences, the shimmering dreams, the power of spirit, combined with the childish sensitiveness and the woeful inefficiency in ordinary matters. They are all perfect. The same delicate satire turns to tragedy in Margaret Kennedy's *Constant Nymph*, but gives similar touches of delicious comment on the absurdities of human temperaments.

Finally, we can always turn back to those jovial old highly peppered and yet enduring satires, *Don Quixote*, *Tom Jones*, *Joseph Andrews*, *Tristram Shandy*, and their kind. Here it is just as important to realize the depth of criticism that at any moment may underlie the robust laughter. Bernard Shaw has never hit more surely the hypocrisy, sentimentality and dogmatism of English respectability than Fielding challenged it in *Tom Jones* and *Joseph Andrews*. And it is a happy incident that has brought back something of *Don Quixote* to Spain today in Unamuno's jovial novel *Mist*, which boxes the compass of the intellectual fads and fashions of the day in the spirit of Cervantes.

The first consideration in the approach to satirical fiction is an important change in attitude. Instead of regarding the satire as a faithful picture of existing conditions anywhere on the globe, we must de-

224

liberately make an allowance for the writer's exaggeration. Whether it be the broad caricature of Dickens or the splashing joke of Mark Twain, or the dainty, barbed wit of Sylvia Warner, or the bitter venom of Samuel Butler and Dean Swift makes no difference in this particular, since the satirist always sees the facts with a marked personal twist in his point of view. Furthermore the twist is usually rooted in the emotion of disgust, contempt, or hatred. They can be almost guaranteed to distort the facts; and yet they often bring out facets of the truth in the distortion, as a caricature suddenly reveals some trait more clearly and luridly than ever before. What should be the reader's attitude in exact terms, then? He should let himself pause, think, and enjoy, but hold a suspended judgment, and always correct the satirical impression by other facts, to get a well-rounded point of view.

Techniques for reading the satirical novel

For example, no reader should miss Butler's *Way of all Flesh*, with its flaming arraignment of the English church of his boyhood. To be disinherited because one cannot enter a particular profession not only represents the dark ages of vocational guidance, but leaves an embittered state of feeling with which we can all sympathize. Moreover, there is an abundance of truth involved in *The Way of all Flesh*, but the truth needs constant correction by reference to outside sources. We must bear in mind that this is the England of the soul-stirring Oxford movement, of Charles Kingsley's tenderness, of Tennyson's *In Memoriam*, of Darwin's first researches, of nineteenth-century liberalism, and the mere reminders will clarify our reading. We shall see at once that the bigotry and cruelty of the Pontifex family cannot possibly represent fixed, usual codes in any inescapable way in that England. They *could* exist, yes. To take them as genuinely representative would be like taking a law against the teaching of evolution as typical of the United States. Fathers and mothers did love their children in the England of 1850. Samuel Butler would never lead us to suspect it, when he endows Ernest's father not only with harshness, but with actual sadistic cruelty.

We have seen that Robert Louis Stevenson re-read Meredith's *Egoist* four times. Re-reading will often be necessary to understand fully the depth of a satire on human society. It will not, however, be so universally necessary to re-read satires as it is in the case of sociological novels, where genuine data in regard to some region are to be collected. Rather in our reading of satirical novels we should simply pause to be sure we see all the involved meanings, and re-read whenever we are doubtful in any way.

Here for the first time in novel-reading we come upon the desirability of memorizing. A pungent aphorism of George Meredith, a mocking bit of raillery from Anatole France, a penetrating satire from Elinor Wylie, a biting epigram of Dean Swift, even a splashing bit from Dickens or Mark Twain will never be outmoded. To enter them in our little omnipresent note-books, to salt them down once for all in memory will be only the work of a moment or two in each case. We have them always ready in the note-book for refreshment if we forget them. Although no bore is more tedious than the one who stampedes our minds with quotations, yet is it not equally true that your brilliant conversationalist knows just where and when to draw upon his supply? Watch the well-known speakers and writers and see how often they whip out their little note-books either surreptitiously or unblushingly to make a note. Needless to say, quotations should always be acknowledged, however lightly.

The evolution of the novel as a historical form is a subject for definite study. It has had a place in the conventional college curriculum for many years, and need not detain us in this connection, since the methods of approach do not differ from those of any other historical inquiry. There is the ancient

The historical evolution of the novel deserves study

oriental tale, the heroic epic, the romance of chivalry, the picaresque adventure, the romance of terror, the novel of manners, the psychological novel, and finally the cult of the subconscious in fiction. All these have intricate ramifying connections with one another, as to periods, fashions, changes, and so on. One form merges into another much as one important dynasty merges into another. There are many key dates and facts to keep in mind. There are many illustrative titles to remember, as well as a vast quantity of material to cover. All of it belongs to the student of literary history, well advanced in the use of literary techniques.

Another form of study is important chiefly for the would-be writer of novels, although it has also some significance for the general reader. This consists in the careful analysis of the writer's processes in his art, his mode of approach to his subject, his techniques in handling the characters, the relation of plot to character, the question of who tells the story, or through whose eyes we shall see it, and so on into many intricate problems of composition. Obviously the young writer will be interested in this type of study.

The analysis of the writer's processes

There are several cautions to be observed here, however. For one thing, the wholesale adaptations of ready-made techniques can be devastating to art, which should always be the natural organic form for a particular subject, growing with it naturally in the writer's mind. The American short story illustrates the elaborate mechanization which can overwhelm the vividness of life and growth. It will not do to study eighteen hundred plots and sub-plots for suggestions. The question rather should be, "What is actually involved in *my* story?" This does not exclude the study of genuine masterpieces for their form, and the enlightenment to be gained from them. They may guide, yes. But to adopt them like a new fashion regardless of one's own subject is fatal.

Secondly, there are no exact and uniform procedures for any art. The history of art is largely a history of violations of codes and cults and rules. Writers themselves do not usually know how they get their effects. Again and again they refer in passing to some hint, some chance remark, some chance observation of a piquant figure, which they noted down in their omnipresent note-books for future treatment. Hawthorne's note-books probably indicate the writer's processes more definitely than any other sources. Yet they are not precise at all in telling us how the seed, dropped into the fertile, imaginative mind, becomes fruit at last.

229

Thirdly, it would seem that much current discussion of the writer's technique is beside the point. For example, the question of who shall appear to tell the story or through whose eyes we shall see it. Whole chapters on the writer's art have been devoted to the thorny problem. Is it really a problem? Does not the reader know all the time that the author is telling his story? That is the unspoken bargain before any reading begins. The question of ways and means to make the story seem true is a highly artificial matter for technicians to discuss. It has never interested the general reader, who will not in any case believe the events to be literally reported. He is not reading the newspaper. All the cloudy discussion of the omniscient author who tells us of matters which his characters could not know or see, goes quite over the reader's head. No sane reader ever supposed that any character of Hardy, or Meredith, or Trollope stopped to survey the landscape as if he were a travel guide. The reader does not resent the author's plain guidance, nor even his attempt to take the points of view of different characters. The only thing that the reader will object to is an inartistic result in the combinations. Nor will the reader believe the story more surely because some one person tells it in the first person singular, like David Copperfield or Henry

Esmond or Pendennis. A flavor of reminiscence
may be very desirable when Pendennis is describing
his old friend, Colonel Newcome. That flavor belongs to art, not to literal verisimilitude. The
importance of it lies only in its appropriateness for
a particular æsthetic effect desired in a particular
instance. Therefore the study of wholesale techniques would seem to have been much overdone,
even by would-be writers. Very noteworthy, also,
is the habit of retirement practised by some of our
best authors. Is it because they wish to develop
their own techniques more quietly?

There is, however, a form of study that will reward
both readers and writers. It is now and then possible to watch the change from literal fact to imaginative idealization. We can watch prosaic details
in their marvellous transmutation into a charmed,
romantic world, and learn at least something of the
process for our guidance.

For example, it is highly instructive to observe the
epic figure of Leatherstocking emerge from Cooper's
first casual reminiscence of an old hunter and trapper
in the pioneer settlement of his boyhood. At first
Leatherstocking is literally translated from memory.
An old relic of the scouting days, he lives on the edge
of the settlement near a ragged, unkempt Indian
known as John Mohican. There is a faint flavor of

social disapproval about them both. Leatherstocking is even haled before the court for violating the game laws. Only at the close of *The Pioneers* do we see the heroic in Leatherstocking, as he calls his dogs for the long trail westward. Such a character would inevitably hate the settlements, so that his escape into the forest is hardly more than literal as yet.

Now Cooper throws his imagination thirty years or so back of his memory, and we have the keen scout, the admired guide, the crack shot, the able leader, Hawkeye, and his Indian friend John Mohican, transformed into the magnificent warrior Chingachgook. There is still nothing inherently improbable here. Hawkeye keeps his homely dialect, his quaint talk about the "red man's gifts", and so on. Another fling of imagination twenty years or so forward from his memory, and we have the fine old trapper of eighty, dying on the prairie, a heroic figure freed from literal fact. In the next novel, *The Pathfinder*, we have Leatherstocking still farther removed from the realism of memory. He is now a full-fledged romantic hero, with notable exploits of leadership and even an unrequited love in the early Victorian manner, very unlike Natty, the simple woodsman. Finally, in the most imaginative stroke of all, we have him as a youth in *Deerslayer*, with his poetic love of the forest, his devotion to the young

Indian chief, Chingachgook, and his simple, ingenuous charm.

Now what is the process which Leatherstocking has undergone in his creator's mind? In so far as we can judge, is it not a constant, steady progress away from literal details of fact into the highly idealized portrait? At first the change represents only the probable one wrought by time, just as we might ask ourselves what any character must have been like twenty or thirty years ago. Then the figure, constantly dwelt upon, takes heroic size in the imagination. He becomes more expressive, more romantic, more poetic. Finally he is the epic embodiment of the pioneer spirit. He represents the truth of an ideal from which the concrete details of reality have dropped away, one by one. He is no longer a literal memory, — the old scout of the settlement as Cooper actually knew him. He is the lure of the forest, the love of the Indian, the bravery of pioneers, the witchery of wooded lakes.

It happens that such a change is thus broadly evident in Cooper's handling of his great subject. We can profitably study similar changes in other novelists. We shall ask ourselves what concrete details of actual experience probably germinated in our author's mind. We cannot follow the hidden process completely, but we can mark the stages

233

where facts drop away to let the living truth of the thought emerge. We can see it sown in weakness and raised in power. General readers will appreciate æsthetic principles more deeply for such questioning, while would-be writers will be stimulated to observe all the wealth of detail about them more closely, to store it away in memory for possible future use.

CHAPTER VIII

THE FRUITS OF READING NOVELS

The values in novel-reading are the intimate values of enriched personality. We become what we are, very largely by our creative reading and by our chosen preferences constantly exercised. Creative reading means reading with active questions in mind, ever on the alert to project new applications from what is read. A single comment from such a reader illuminates any text, while we have all squirmed under the "total recall" of the passive reader.

The enrichment of personality

The warmth of personal preference stimulates this creative attitude in reading. We not only absorb more readily, but we throw out comment, suggestion, illustration, appreciation in a much more lively way if we are *en rapport* with our author. Hundreds of students have shown this fact in our classes. Therefore we should pay very serious regard to our personal preferences in reading. Tastes can be cultivated, it is true, but the cultivation will be more quickly and surely achieved along the lines of our natural growth.

It is probable that when we are *en rapport* with a favorite author, there is some special correspondence of temperament which makes our appreciations peculiarly vivid, apt, and immediate. Such moods cannot be seized with too much zest. Browsing and re-reading will emphasize the influence and make our authors into old friends, although much browsing is simple recalling rather than re-reading.

One has only to turn to distinguished writers to see how their reading has influenced their personalities, and developed them. There is no need for Henry James to tell us how he admired Balzac, "the master of us all", and Turgenev, "the beautiful genius." We should know without being told that Edith Wharton has studied Flaubert, Maupassant, Chekov, Balzac, and her master, Henry James. We should know in any case that Conrad studied Henry James for twenty years, and that Willa Cather has read much of James. We could guess without difficulty that Arnold Bennett has read the Russian novelists with admiration. We are not surprised that Nietsche regarded Dostoiefsky as one of the happiest windfalls of his life.

Anatole France has left us one of the prettiest stories of early influences in reading in his exquisite little tale "*Le Livre de mon Ami.*" The "ami" is no less than his past self, a little fellow crossing the

236

Luxembourg Gardens as a day-boy on his way to an old school when the leaves of the plane trees are falling on the statues in October. What rare books, prints, curios to be had from the book stalls of the quays! What memories of absorbed reading on the way home, by the flaring shop windows in the narrow streets of the faubourg! Some passages in the classics always retain the flavor of such evenings for the little fellow. So absorbed is he that he sometimes collides with the pastry cook's boy carrying the huge hamper on his head, and stops absently by the lantern of the chestnut-vendor to read.

Reading like this is more than taking in facts. It is vivid, vicarious experience for children, so that some of us, when we think of David Copperfield, find it difficult to believe that we did not ourselves in some other life stand at the gate bidding the mother good-bye. It is not as if we had read it, but once lived it. And in very truth we live many lives in the novels to which we give ourselves.

The enrichment of personality would be lost without social interchange. We carry our enrichment with us. And how evident it becomes! It would probably be somewhat mechanical to point our reading directly towards social intercourse. Yet the fruits are there and will bring us rewarding contacts inevi-

The enrichment of social intercourse

tably. Probably, too, it would do most of us no harm to review briefly the best novels we are reading, with the most seasoned, pungent comments we can make upon them, before we take dinner with friends, or even with our families.

Finally, there is something much more important than personal enrichment, or even contact with our **Identifi-** immediate circle. We shall not touch **cation** many human beings personally. Even a **with** Kreisler, a Lloyd George, an Edison, a **humanity** Lindbergh, touches only special groups on the earth. Moreover, most of us are absurdly class-bound, race-bound, haunted by a motley crew of prejudices, old clichés, sentimental, stereotyped concepts, and unwarranted, shuddering distastes. With the best novels of all nations in our hands we can feel a vast sweep of interested sympathy that will include the coolie stevedore, the untouchable on his mat, the miner, the farm-hand, the hobo, and the engineer. We shall know how it feels to work in the damp, hot jungle, and the dark, wind-swept snows of the Nordland in Scandinavia. We shall not stop short of identification with humanity itself. This will be the last, prized, autumnal fruit of our reading.